BEFORE YOU BUY THAT

PUPPY

All inquiries should be addressed to:
Barron's Educational Series, Inc.
250 Wireless Boulevard
Hauppauge, New York 11788

Library of Congress Catalog Card No. 93-40219

International Standard Book No. 0-8120-1750-1

Library of Congress Cataloging-in-Publication Data

Wrede, Barbara, 1931-
    Before you buy that puppy / Barbara J. Wrede.
        p.   cm.
    Includes bibliographical references (p.   ) and index.
    ISBN 0-8120-1750-1
    1. Dogs. 2. Puppies. 3. Dogs—Buying. I. Title.
SF426.W74   1994
636.7'0887—dc20   93-40219
                                             CIP

PRINTED IN HONG KONG
67   9927   9876543

BEFORE YOU BUY THAT

PUPPY

with 82 Photographs

Barbara J. Wrede

BARRON'S

Photo Credits
Donna Coss: front cover, inside front cover (top left), pages iv (center), v (top middle, center left and right),1, 3, 4, 17 (top), 21 (top), 22 (top), 25, 29, 32 (bottom), 71, back cover; Michele Earle-Bridges: inside front cover (bottom left), pages 9, 10, 17 (bottom), 29, 31, 36 (top), 40, 44, 45, 52, 75, 76, 80, 85, 87; Aaron Norman: pages v (top right), 21 (bottom), 24, 32 (top), 33, 68, inside back cover (top left); Judith Strom: inside front cover (top right, bottom right), pages iv (top left and right, center right, bottom left and right), v (top left, bottom left and right), 7, 14, 18, 19, 20, 22 (bottom), 23, 27, 30, 34, 36 (bottom), 37, 41, 56, 57, 58, 59, 62, 65, 66, 69, 77, 78, 79, 83, 88, 90, inside back cover (top right, bottom); Barbara Wrede: pages x, 2, 67.

The Photos on Pages iv and v
Page iv—top left: Labrador retriever puppy; top right: Brittany spaniel puppy; center: papillon; center right: German shepherd puppies; bottom left: chow-chow puppies; bottom right: Border collie. Page v— top left: Doberman pinscher; top middle: Australian shepherd puppy; top right: Shih Tzu; center left: Shar-pei puppies; center right: Samoyeds; bottom left: German shepherd puppy; bottom right: Anatolian shepherd puppy.

About the Author
Barbara J. Wrede has lived with puppies and dogs all her life. The cocker spaniels of her young years were replaced first by boxers, then by weimaraners, and finally by a multitude of Great Danes. Wrede has held obedience training classes for all breeds of dogs, but more significantly, she has spent hours helping puppy and dog owners solve canine training problems that threatened the optimum bonding between dog and owner. While she was actively breeding and selling dogs, she compiled many pages of training and care suggestions for people all over North America who had obtained puppies from her. Those personal recipes for living happily with puppies were the genesis of *Civilizing Your Puppy*. Her years of experience in helping people select a puppy, both as a breeder and as a volunteer at animal shelter and rescue organizations, underlie the advice given in this book.

Acknowledgments
I would like to thank my editor, Don Reis, who is a joy to work with. I'm also grateful to all the people who talked to me honestly about their dogs so I could tell it the way it really is in discussing various breeds. Finally, thanks to my husband, Kent, who always understands when the book comes first.

Note
This book deals with the acquisition and keeping of dogs. The publisher considers it important to point out that the rules fo dog keeping set forth in this book apply primarily to normally developed young dogs from a good breeder, that is, to healthy animals with good character traits. Owing to bad experiences with humans, some dogs may have peculiar behavior or may tend to bite. These dogs should be taken in only by experienced dog owners. Even well-trained and carefully supervised dogs may cause damage to someone else's property or even cause accidents. Sufficient insurance coverage is in your own interest. In any case, taking out a dog liability policy for your pet is strongly recommended.

Contents

Foreword

It's difficult to imagine life without dogs, though there are a few places in the world where our faithful companions have been banished. As far back as we can trace human history, there dogs have been, too—partners, companions, and helpers to people. I know of no creature but the dog who will do so much for so little—a kind word, a pat on the head, a square meal, and the privilege of sharing whatever you call home are the dog's reward.

Unfortunately, for too many dogs the return is abuse and abandonment. Literally millions of dogs are killed at animal shelters in the United States every year, and it's tempting to say those are the lucky ones among the canine losers. More thousands are thrown out of vehicles along the roads or just left behind when their owners move on. In the hells known as puppy mills, dogs live in squalor and misery, cranking out litter after litter of puppies and killed when their "useful" days are done. Dogs suffer vivisection needlessly; how many times do people need to cut spinal cords to know what nerve responses still go on? Yet many schools still participate in cruel "experiments," the outcomes of which have been known for decades.

All abandoned dogs were once someone's cute puppy. Heedless people still allow female dogs to produce litters of puppies for no better reason than for "the children to see the miracle of birth." Then let those same children see the miracle of death, too, in the killing rooms of shelter after shelter across this country where the unwanted and rejected puppies go.

The little Dutch boy put his finger into the hole in the dike to keep his land from flooding. This book is my finger in the dike. If I am useful in guiding some people not to get a puppy, I will consider my aim met. If I can persuade some people to rescue some of the wonderful dogs that wait in our crowded shelters and give them loving homes, I'll be delighted. If this book is a reliable guide for finding the dog of your dreams, who will happily live all its life with you, I've done my job.

Fortuna, California
June, 1993

Chapter 1
Reality Check Time

The New Is Not the Old

When my friend Mary had to put her old poodle to sleep, the decision was inescapably agonizing. Afterward, Mary found a dogless life cold indeed. So, at age 83, she went and got herself a poodle puppy.

The puppy was a disaster! Accustomed to her sedate old companion, Mary was far from ready for the demands of a rambunctious youngster. The puppy did everything normal puppies do. It chewed on the furniture. It gnawed on Mary's slippers. It piddled on the rugs. It hassled the cat. It didn't know about coming when called, so Mary spent more time than she wanted to out in the cold and the dark waiting for the puppy to get tired of flitting around the yard and come indoors.

Far from taking her life back to the happy days she remembered with her old dog, the new puppy made Mary's life a merry hell— merry for the puppy, and hell for Mary. Finally her daughter, who sized up the bad match between

Standard poodles have brains, stamina, and a desire to please.

her mother and the puppy, took it off her mother's hands.

Realizing now that she wasn't capable of the same activity that she had been when her old dog was a puppy, Mary made a wise decision. She found a breeder who had a two-year-old poodle and brought home the adult dog. Basically housebroken and responsive to simple commands like "Come" and "Sit," the new dog needed only fine-tuning to fit into Mary's home and way of life. Week by week the poodle becomes more

1

One of the author's harlequin Great Danes playing in the river.

"Good Advice" Often Isn't

Whenever people are mourning the death of a beloved old dog, the conventional wisdom is that they should immediately get a puppy that closely resembles the dog they've lost. While this strategy may work sometimes, I suspect that more often than not, it doesn't. One reason for the high failure rate is that no two dogs are alike—even relatives of the same breed. I still remember learning that lesson. I had to have my dear old black Great Dane, Sapphire, put to sleep on a workday morning. When I got home that afternoon, I went to a corner and did some more bawling. Kent, my husband, discovered me there when he arrived home.

"Is there anything I can do?" he asked.

I sniffled, "Yes. Go to the kennels and bring in Cappy." Cappy was Sapphire's big black son, a lovable goof. If I couldn't have Sapphire, I reasoned, I'd find comfort in her son.

True to his nature, Cappy came galumphing into the house, greeted me effusively, gave the house cats a short lesson in evasive tactics, swiped a cube of butter off the kitchen counter, found a toy, and recruited me for a game of fetch-the-ball. All evening, Cappy kept me busy.

All the next morning, Cappy kept me busy. Ditto all that afternoon.

like the dear old companion Mary lived with for so long. Mary delights in finding ways in which the new dog is, she says, brighter than her old one.

Because she has a perceptive daughter who forcefully intervened, Mary has been spared the unhappiness many people experience when they get puppies they can't cope with. Too often the outcomes are much more unhappy. Either the puppy is permanently banished to the end of a chain in the backyard, or it is taken to an animal shelter, where it has one chance in ten of being adopted. Those not adopted will be killed; in the United States, at least 15 million dogs and cats are killed in animal shelters each year.

Not only isn't the new puppy the equivalent of the old dog; more importantly, people don't realize how much *their* lives have changed since their dog was a pup.

And evening. It wasn't that he was deliberately giving me grief therapy by taking my mind off the loss of Sapphire. Cappy was a very busy Dane, whereas his mother had been mellow and quiet. Sapphire was always there for me, but unobtrusively. Cappy wanted to be in on every joke and was available all the time. He was a delight, but not 24 hours a day every day. I needed some relief—time when he visited other Danes out in his pen.

After three days of Cappy's antics, I cheerfully took him back to his pen and brought a quieter Dane into the house for awhile. As I did so, I thought deeply about the truth that in no way can you really replace one dog with another. Over many years of raising and selling Great Danes and hearing people's stories of grief, I concluded that it's usually better to get a puppy that is different in some obvious way from the dog. If your Dane was black, then try a blue or a harlequin. If you're mourning a female, get a male puppy. Change the circumstances enough so that the moment-to-moment comparisons aren't valid, and the healing process goes forward at a faster pace.

To be honest, shortly after I wrote this passage, I realized that I was sabotaging myself by trying to replace Pinocchio, a lovely and loving harlequin Dane I had been mourning for nearly two years. There was not a harlequin Dane on

the entire West Coast who lived up to Pinocchio, and I continued dogless until I read what I had written. Then, in a fit of sanity, I got Cordy, a spectacular blue male Dane who is as unlike Pinocchio as a skateboard is to a Lamborghini.

Moreover, conventional wisdom doesn't take into account the changes that happen to people. As with Mary, we're all older than we were the last time we civilized a puppy. In the first five or six decades of our lives, another ten or twelve years is no big deal. In the seventh, eighth, or ninth decades, though, our athletic abilities begin to ebb, and puppies may be more than we're up to.

It may even be that at some point we decide that our favorite breed is more dog than we can handle. I can see Opal, a wonderful breeder of Great Danes, ringside at a show one fall day. In her arms was a papillon.

"Look at this," Opal said, stroking the dog's silky coat. "Did

Like all their relatives, these Norwich terriers will grow into feisty bundles of energy.

you ever expect to see me with something like this?"

After I had agreed that a papillon was a departure from Dane, Opal said, "I just realized one day that I no longer have the vigor it takes to show Danes. I'll always have a house Dane, but from now on, my dog showing will be with something easy, like a papillon."

Another major life change happens when people retire. Free now from the workday week, many people choose to travel. In campground after campground, I've seen retired people with small dogs, compact travel companions that fit nicely into a camper or a motor home. Many of these folks tell me that they used to own larger dogs but decided that when they were going to be on the road a lot of the time, smaller pets were more sensible.

At another point on the career spectrum, some people get very involved in their work. Having spent their apprenticeships doing jobs they didn't care about very much and at which they could put in the minimum daily requirement, they're now moving up the career ladder. With increased responsibility often come increased hours at the job. Where once their beloved dog was at home alone for a nine-to-five stint, now the poor dog is having to spend ten and twelve hours a day in solitary. People at that point in their lives don't need the conventional wisdom of "Replace your old dog with a new puppy." They need to consider whether they'll have a dog at all, at least until they begin to slow down at work.

And with a changing economy, in most families both adults have jobs outside the home, so the old stereotype of Mom staying at home to raise the kids, puppy, guppies, and hamsters is out of date. When Mom has a three-hour commute on top of an eight-hour workday, she's not up for chasing puppies or cleaning hamster cages when she gets home.

Cute Is Not Enough

Have you ever seen an ugly puppy? Ugly dogs, yes, but puppies, no matter what they're going to become, are generally cute. That's why it's so treacherous to send a darling little curly-headed kid to the mall with a box of fuzzy, cute puppies that no one really wants. The package of kid plus pups is the best sales device on earth. It takes a hard heart, indeed—or a very cool head—to walk past and not be a pushover for the cute little furballs.

"Free puppies!" says the hand-lettered sign.

Well, there ain't no free lunch, and there's no such thing as a free puppy, either! Forget for the moment shots, and neutering, and vets' bills, and food, and toys. Just concentrate on what it takes to bring that cute puppy along to a sensible, trained, adult dog. Just think time, and energy, and emotional attachment, and guilt. Free? Not by a long shot.

Recently, a man I know was exclaiming about how much time and energy my friend spends on her poodle.

"I've never really known a dog before," he said.

This man has adult children, and I thought it strange that, given his background, those children had never had pets. So I asked him about that.

"Oh," he said, surprised, "yeah, the kids always had a dog around. But I never remember doing anything about it."

Oh, yeah. Twenty-five years ago there was a wife at home who took care of things like civilizing the puppy the kids brought home from the mall. *Somebody* did something about the family dog!

Dogs and Puppies Seldom Make Good Gifts

When Kent and I were raising Great Danes and selling puppies, one of the things we drew the line on was the "Christmas puppy." Oh, yes, we did sometimes have pups available around December, but I refused to let one of them go to its new home on Christmas Eve or Christmas Day. Instead, I urged adults who wanted the "Christmas puppy" to place books about Great Danes under the tree, as well as toys appropriate to a Dane puppy, and perhaps new food dishes. Certainly a photo of the puppy coming to that house just as soon as the hysteria of Christmas was over was an item not to be overlooked.

But not the actual, flesh-and-blood puppy.

How come? Think of the uproar of Christmas, especially with children. Consider the comings and goings, the tree taking up space, the packages a puppy can get into, the relatives leaving doors open so a puppy can run out into the street and get killed, the stress and tension. What kind of introduction is that for a puppy? Its new home is in chaos, and it doesn't even know who lives there!

Far, far better to spend holiday time talking about the puppy, explaining the use of each item for the new puppy, discussing names for the puppy, getting in good lessons about how the puppy is a lot like a baby and needs certain care and teaching, and finishing with who will be responsible for what. Then, when the visitors have departed, when the children have played with all their new toys, and peace falls gently upon the hearth again, it's time for the puppy to come home. The children have learned that a puppy is not a toy that comes in a box under the tree, and preoccupied adults haven't had to integrate a new member into the family at a busy time.

Nor do I believe a puppy—or a dog—should be given to anyone on any holiday unless the recipient is absolutely amenable to receiving such a gift. When we talk about pets, we're talking about shared lives. The person who's going to be the primary sharer ought to have all the say as to what kind of puppy or dog—and when. Yes, parents are the ones to decide the children are old enough and responsible enough to have a family dog. And yes, sometimes we need to push our elderly relatives into getting a pet to reinvolve them in life. But too many of the puppies and dogs that end up in the killing rooms of animal shelters were basically unwanted gifts, unsuited to the situation, and treated as objects instead of as the living beings they are, requiring and deserving love and care.

It's no accident that good animal shelters refuse to let a person adopt a pet for someone else.

Experience has proved that the match works best when the person who's going to live with the dog picks it out. When you get to the section of this book that describes special dogs, such as Seeing Eye dogs, you'll find that much care goes into qualifying each recipient for exactly the right dog.

The only person you can properly gift with a puppy is yourself!

So How Do I Decide to Get a Puppy?

In spite of the warnings I've given, I'd find my world bleak were there never again a puppy in it, and in this I'm not unique. Let's run a checklist—a check of current reality—and see where puppies fit in, as well as what kind of puppies to consider. In Chapter 2 I'll specifically discuss many different kinds of dogs; so here I'll deal just with generalities as far as breeds go.

1. Whose Puppy Will It Be?

Children: A time-honored idea is that all children need a puppy. To a certain extent, it's true that children and puppies thrive together. However, the children must be old enough to understand how to behave toward another living creature. The best way to decide whether a child is ready for a puppy is to note how she or he interacts with dogs of your relatives or friends. The child that plays gently and lovingly with a dog and begs for its own dog is probably ready. However, choose carefully, for many puppies of tiny breeds are too fragile for young children. Interestingly, big puppies of the working and herding groups of dogs are rarely rough with small children. Their basic nature is to protect their people, and they extend that guardianship to a gentleness with little people.

Elderly Relatives: We are learning more and more that pets keep older people active, responsive, and involved with life; and, as more of us have aging parents, the temptation is to get a puppy for an elderly parent or friend. Mary's experience, though, is one we all might heed. While the silliness of a puppy is an excellent antidote to the aches of arthritis, it's vital that the person getting the puppy is able to cope with it.

There is a thoughtful compromise between foisting a puppy on a person perhaps not able to cope and giving an adult dog. Instead, volunteer time every day to help the older person civilize the gift puppy. That way everyone shares the fun of seeing a puppy grow and learn, and the older person isn't stuck with a taxing gift.

Here, too, choosing the right kind of puppy is crucial. Little terriers and poodles, for instance, amuse themselves very well in the confines of a house and get plenty of exercise. This is a consideration, for many older people aren't up to the kind of exercise that many sporting dogs, for instance, need for happy lives. In

A Belgian Malinois and a child play serious tug-of-war.

the section on dogs for special needs (see pages 55–63), you'll learn more about making the right match of pet and person.

Family: The family dog sleeping by the hearth, one eye open to make sure all is well, is one of those Norman Rockwell pictures most of us get sentimental over—as well we might. But to get a dog to that point of serenity takes choosing the right pup to begin with. Then, it takes all kinds of family cooperation during the training process. Though few puppies refuse to be family dogs at adulthood, some breeds are more oriented toward bonding with only one person. Such dogs can be forced to accept other family members, but why put everyone through the trouble? Check out the many kinds of dogs there are, what they were bred to do, and pick one that the family can agree on that falls into the category of "good with a whole family." One of the basic rules of living well with puppies and dogs is to choose intelligently for the life you have in mind for yourself and your dog. You're not going to be a champion duck hunter with a chihuahua, and you're getting more than you bargained for if you choose a Saint Bernard to be your frail old auntie's lap dog.

Yourself: Twelve years ago my friend Tom chose Toby, a golden retriever puppy, as his own dog. Through many, many moves and job changes, through good times and bad, Tom and Toby have been a team. Golden retrievers are generally known for their friendliness with everyone, and Toby is no exception, being a fine visitor and having his own special friends he likes to see. But Toby has gone beyond being everyone's dog. He is bonded, first, last, and always with Tom. Though he may rest quietly in my house while Tom goes out to get something from his car, Toby sets up a yodel that can be heard in the whole neighborhood if Tom so much as runs to the store for a container of milk and leaves him behind. He's a good example of how close the bond between dog and person can be, and he's many people's dream dog.

You could choose one of the even more personally oriented dogs if you wish. The chow comes to mind first as a breed that chooses its person and then ignores the rest of the human race. For a person who chooses not to live with other people, such a puppy is a wonderful companion. But such a puppy also poses a big responsibility. In adulthood the dog will suffer and even die if separated from its chosen human companion. When I was volunteering at our humane society shelter, a chow came in. His owner, a navy man, had been transferred. There was a mix-up in the transfer, and the quarters in which the man could keep his dog with him were not available. That chow refused to eat. He ignored every one of us at the shelter, even when we went into his cage and sat and petted him. He was in deep mourning. Most fortunately, his man was unusually committed to his dog and raised a ruckus I can only imagine. Two weeks after he had been committed to the shelter, skin and bones as he was, the chow joyfully welcomed his owner and the two of them left to continue their life together.

So before you choose a dog to bond with you and only you, look carefully at your life for the next ten or fifteen years. Will you be able to keep your end of the bargain?

2. How Much Time Do I Have for Training?

I've successfully housebroken puppies in three days. Those have been three days of not doing much else except keeping an eye on the puppy.

Furthermore, they have to be three *continuous* days or the lessons are forgotten. But it can be done. Do you have three days to give to this venture? And what happens after that? I've always been lucky enough to have had jobs where I could free up a good chunk of time, so I've chosen to start new puppies when I was free of the day-to-day demands of the job.

True, almost everyone gets vacation. But do you want a puppy badly enough to spend your vacation at home training it? Training must be done at home, you know, because lessons learned elsewhere may not carry over to home. If you are willing to stay home, spending a vacation training and bonding with a new puppy is an outstanding way to get an excellent start on your life together. It's an investment of time and energy you'll appreciate for years.

However, puppy training isn't like a flu shot—do it once a year and everything will be okay. Dogs are social animals, even the ones that want to socialize with only one person. All dogs suffer when they must spend most of their time alone. So if vacation is the only time all year when the dog will have companionship, it isn't fair to get a puppy. If, however, you're considering a family dog, determine how much time some member of the family will be at home. With today's shifting patterns of family life, a welcoming dog might indeed be great comfort to a child who comes home several hours before the parents do.

3. Is My Home Equal to What a Puppy Can Do to It?

I have a strong bias about where dogs live. They are domesticated

Training is an on-going process.

animals, trained and bred for centuries to share our lives with us. From the time they first shared our ancestors' hearths, they have shown a wonderful willingness to adapt to whatever ups and downs our lives go through. They seem not to mind if we have to move up to a palace or down to a shanty, as long as they can share with us. With very few exceptions, their nature is that they want to share with us.

No dog was ever intended, by breeding or nature, to spend its life on the end of a chain, its only shelter some box and its only companionship the occasional appearance of some human who drops food in front of it.

So when I bring up the question of whether your house is up to what a puppy can do to it, I'm serious, because I expect that your puppy is going to spend the greatest part of its life in your house with you. In my book *Civilizing Your Puppy* I share many tips on how to teach a puppy to live acceptably in your house with you. I certainly agree that everyone, human and canine, needs to have personal time and space. But if you live alone, for instance, and work long days, where can a puppy safely stay while you're teaching it to be a mannerly member of your family? This might bring you to consider an adult dog rather than a puppy. Many serious breeders of purebred dogs do have adult dogs that they're willing to sell. Perhaps a show puppy that didn't pan out might be available, or maybe they have more dogs than they really want at the moment. Another source of adult dogs is your local humane society shelter. At most of them, staff and volunteers work closely with dogs that are brought in, to discover which can adjust to a new home. You can learn a lot about the dog's temperament and quirks from the personnel at the shelter. Visit with the dog, take it for a walk, and get to know it. Form

Irish setters need a lot of exercise.

your own opinions, as well as learning all you can from the people who've been caring for the dog. I've had several shelter dogs and have been happy with all of them.

4. What's My Energy Level?

Here again we face the decision—puppy or adult dog? If you are under stress yet would dearly love to have a delightful corgi to welcome you home at night, maybe you'd be better off getting a corgi whom someone has already turned into a delight! There's no stigma about admitting that you have neither the energy nor the will to turn a a nuttsy puppy into a dignified, sedate borzoi. So if it's a sedate borzoi you want, go get one—an adult.

And by the way, forget the nonsense about not being able to teach anything to an adult dog. Just like us, dogs like to learn and they appreciate the challenge of new lessons. Furthermore, an adult dog will love you and thank you in direct proportion to how much you, yourself, give love and a good home. There's a lot of misinformation about being able to bond only with puppies. Yes, there are some things you'll miss if you don't have your dog from puppyhood, but many of those a lot of us could do without very well. I could have skipped the day when Kent remarked as we were cleaning up the rug, "Wow! It isn't every day that you can clean up after a puppy and his grandfather all on the same day!" And I could have done without the day when I had to call in sick because my current puppy had just eaten my last pair of good shoes.

5. How Stable Will My Life Be in the Near Future?

I live in an area where there are two colleges. In May and June our local animal shelter bulges with abandoned dogs and cats, left behind by students going home, going to Europe—leaving without the pet they so eagerly took on in the autumn. Remember the statistics—an estimated 15 million friendly, healthy dogs and cats killed in 1992 because there weren't homes for them!

Kittens and puppies, dogs and cats are not disposable tissues. A pet is a responsibility, sometimes a drain. I strongly advise all who are at an early stage of building their adult life to stay unattached as far as pets are concerned. Housing rentals where one may have pets are hard to find. When seeking about in the job market, one must be ready to move around, often long distances. Tom is unusually committed to Toby, and he has had to make some dreadful housing choices in order to have Toby with him. It's hard on a dog to be constantly moving around, and many develop strange behavior problems as a result of their insecurity.

When we're ready to settle down, there will be time for puppies and for faithful old dogs that have grown gray and creaky sharing our less bouncy lives. If you're in a state of constant moving, pass by that cute kid with the darling puppies at the mall. What you have to offer now isn't fit for a dog!

6. What Other Pet Might I Consider?

As a matter of fact, when Tom was in college, he had fish. He delighted in confounding people by taking his fish, in their bowl, for occasional bicycle rides! When you read "No pets" in a for-rent ad, generally fish aren't included in the ban. Fish are restful, interesting, beautiful, portable, and not prone to behavior problems if you change residences frequently.

They bridge the gap between having nothing living to look forward to at home and having a miserable, emotionally neglected dog that makes you feel guilty every time it whines in sorrow when you have to go to work.

People who don't know cats think that they do not suffer from not having their people around, but they do. However, cats are more able to amuse themselves than dogs are; if you live where it's safe for cats to go outside, cats keep themselves pretty busy. But cats are still domesticated and they flourish from having their people around. Two cats do better than one if they have to be alone a lot. However, cats are not pack or group animals. Some like other cats; some don't. In our family, we have some cats that like their dogs a lot better than they like each other.

Exotic birds are popular pets, and they have certain advantages over dogs. They don't need to be exercised, they flourish indoors, most landlords have no bans on them, and they're easily contained. However, birds make very strong bonds and need the company of the person/people they've bonded with. Left alone, they become neurotic, pull their feathers out, peck themselves, don't eat, get sick, and die. So birds are a fine choice for pets if space or energy is at a premium, but they're a very poor choice if time is the problem.

In general, fad pets are a bad idea. We all saw the rise of little pigs as household pets. They were advertised as smarter than dogs, cleaner than cats, and the wonder discovery of the decade. Many of them grew too big to be kept comfortably in the average house or apartment, and often their dispositions soured as their people grew disappointed in them. Every animal shelter in the country could probably tell you their favorite pig horror story by now, as the cute little piglets grew up, grew cranky, and got dumped by their owners who hadn't had bacon in mind in the beginning!

Equally bad ideas are exotics. Friends had a monkey. Whee! I'd always wanted a monkey for a pet until I got to know that one, which, as monkeys go, was a nice monkey. Destructive, demanding, dangerous (she bit fiercely), and dirty, she was a real pain. My friends took good care of her and kept her because they are people who take commitments seriously, but they would never have another. I was quickly cured of wanting any monkeys in my life! One of my college professors had an ocelot who ate the baby's toes. The stories are legion, all with one message: Dogs and cats have been domesticated and make excellent pets under the right circumstances. The other animals have chosen a different life path, and forcing them into pseudo-domestication is iffy at best and often dangerous.

But I Still Want a Puppy

Good. You've run the reality checklist and the answer still comes up "Puppy." In the next chapter, let's examine the various breeds available and see what their hallmarks are.

Chapter 2
Choices, Choices

Actually, I don't even think every puppy is cute! I've seen nervous, sharp-toothed, practically hairless puppies of dubious ancestry leaping and yapping at everyone that comes near them, and I've been able to pass them up as potential life companions without hesitation. Maybe my puppy-judging eye is sensitized by knowledge of what some puppies are going to be when they grow up. I see the future dog in that puppy, and I don't want that dog. Obviously, considering our crowded animal shelters, I'm not alone in steering clear of some dogs. However, I really believe there's the right person for every puppy, and what I'd like to do in this chapter is help you see the dog in the puppy. This might help you make your initial choice one that you can live with happily—and long.

The Myth of the Mixed-breed

"The best dogs," people assure me solemnly, "are the mixed-breeds."

Sometimes that's true. Sometimes a happy accident of genes produces a dog of superior intelligence, amenable to socializing, of sturdy health and pleasing body type. Joli was such a dog. He was a cross between a setter and a cocker spaniel, a slender, medium-coated, black dog who, as a puppy, licked my face and snuggled down into my jacket with a happy sigh that overcame all the sensible reasons against my having a dog. I lived alone on the third floor of an apartment building that fronted on the town's main street and backed onto the fishing docks. I worked full time. I was barely making both ends meet.

And Joli, with the oldest puppy trick in the book, won me in an instant. I overcame all obstacles, using the fire escape landing outside my only window as Joli's "yard," padding it with weighted-down newspapers so he could do his potty out there, and keeping a chair by the window so he could clamber out by himself as he grew. Soon he was agile enough to manage the fire escape steps by himself. On cold or rainy days, Joli

This Lab mixed-breed is an eager companion on daily walks.

went one flight up to the flat roof to do his potty, chase seagulls, and bark down four stories at startled passersby on the street. On nice days he scampered around the docks and the parking lot abutting them.

He not only scampered around, Joli also stole! Not until I heard a shouted "Come back here, you son of a gun!," heavy footsteps running up the fire escape, and saw Joli sail in through the window with a lunch sack in his mouth did I realize what his morning outings included. The fisherman who appeared at my window a few paces behind Joli explained that the men brought extras for Joli, but that lately he had

taken to helping himself to any lunch that caught his olfactory fancy. To stop his stealing, Joli subsequently had to go on his morning outings under my supervision, and my window had to be closed when I went to work. But we managed. I also was young and agile, and three flights of fire escape were no problem.

However, as he matured, Joli developed a real wanderlust. I had left the docks and had a house in the country. It was a simpler time, safer for dogs and for people, and I let Joli run loose when I was at home, more or less keeping my eye on him. If, first thing in the morning, I saw Joli maneuvering along our long driveway toward the lane and called him to come back into his yard, he did so willingly, even acting hurt that I seemed to suspect him of planning a sneak. For the rest of the day I could count on Joli's being in his own yard. But if I missed that first sneak of the day, Joli was happily off on his regular circuit. From a friend who lived about five miles away I began to learn Joli's route.

"He gets to me around 10:00 in the morning," she told me, "and scratches at the screen door. If I have a bone for him, I give it to him and off he goes. If I have nothing, I pat him, he wags his tail, and trots away."

Intrigued, I checked with other local friends. Indeed, my dog had a route with about a five-mile circumference. He politely panhandled all along his route, had a number of friends I hadn't met before, and was well received. Everyone appreciated his nice disposition and the fact that he didn't hassle other animals.

It was, as I said, a simpler time. Nice dogs roaming in the country were in minimal danger. If they caused no damage, people in those less litigious times tended to ignore them—or even give them handouts. Traffic was moderate, and Joli mostly went crosslots. So the story of Joli and his roving ways is one of those sentimental tales of times past that feed the myth of the ideal mongrel, beloved by all who knew him.

As a matter of fact, today if Joli didn't get me fined to within an inch of my life by the animal control people or sued for much more than I'm worth, he'd get shot by a touchy property owner or mangled by traffic. Sweet, stubborn Joli with his wandering ways would have to be penned or constantly supervised these days, and his story would be far less interesting—or heart-tugging!

Nor did I have any way of knowing that the cute puppy I took would grow up to be an amiable panhandler. The problem with a mixed-breed puppy is that no one can tell what the adult is going to be like. Dainty little puppy paws tell us that the adult won't be very big. Coat length is more difficult to judge. But the really opaque part is the core of the dog: What temperament will this pup develop?

Even from the same litter, mixed-breed puppies vary widely in looks and personality. And some mixed-breedings produce just awful dogs.

You haven't lived until you're running an obedience class and in walks a spindly teenager on the other end of the leash from a 130-pound (59 kg) Akita-German shepherd cross who has but one aim in life—to take your face off! In your book of infamy, mark down also Prince, the so-called miniature German Shepherd who bit everyone in range, including his owner, and went into hysterics whenever anyone tried to curb him.

One reason we see as many fine mixed-breed dogs as we do is that nature is pretty smart about mutations. The really dreadful mutations are usually lethal. Another reason we see some okay mixed-breeds is that natural selection is often allowed to operate with a mixed-breed litter. Humans generally don't interfere with an unwanted litter of mixed-breed pups, and the weak or unfit ones die early. The survivors have at least a modicum of health. Finally, of the mixed-breed puppies that wind up at animal shelters, those with nasty dispositions or puny constitutions are killed, not offered for adoption. So what you get to choose from are the most promising of the lot, though no one still can be sure how the pups will turn out. Shelter workers often have to guess wildly at the parentage of mixed-breed puppies.

Thus, in choosing a mixed-breed puppy, what you see is not necessarily what you'll get. If you're up for surprises, some of which are pleasant, then taking on a mixed-breed

Many mongrels grow into fine, beloved dogs.

puppy is an adventure. There is less adventure in adopting an adult mixed-breed, for by then personality traits have shown themselves. Shelter workers get to know the adult dogs they offer for adoption and can tell you a lot about how the dog behaves, approaches people, and interacts with other dogs. Even so, there may be surprises, for the shelter is a stressful environment and a dog will change once it's in a home where it's loved and secure. Later I'll talk about the special needs of shelter dogs when they're adopted.

The Predictability Factor

Be aware that now as I go on to discuss the characteristics of specific purebred dogs, I am *not* saying that no one should ever decide on a mixed-breed dog as their pet. But

purebred dogs from breeders who know, love, and value the standard for that breed are predictable as no mixed-breed dogs can be.

For every pure breed of dog, there is a written standard that not only describes what dogs of that breed should look like, but often also spells out what the dogs' personalities should be. Great Danes, the dogs I know best, are supposed to be gentle and steady with their families, fearless, and calm. Dane puppies showing too much aggressiveness, an unwillingness to be trained, or fearful shyness should be humanely put to sleep. People can't live with 150-pound (68 kg) fear-biters. Though it's hard, breeders who care deeply about the dogs to whom they're committed do follow their breed standard and do, in fact, cull to the standard. In a careful, intelligent breeding program such culling is rarely necessary, because only dogs displaying the correct breed traits are used as parents.

So when you decide on a purebred puppy, what you see is, within a knowable spectrum, what you'll get. Your training program for the dog can enhance or suppress certain qualities, but you can know what you have to work with. In Chapter 3, I'll fill you in on what to look for in a breeder so you can assess whether the person is truly breeding to the standard, trying to make a fast buck, or flying blind.

Now let's look at what dogs you might choose for what folks.

A Puppy for the Children

Good natured and sturdy are two essential qualities that immediately come to mind when I think of a puppy for children. I'd recommend medium-sized to large dogs, because these can participate in the romping children like with their dogs. I'd certainly avoid dogs known for hair-trigger tempers, as I would also avoid dogs noted for runnng off. Here I'll talk about several very popular breeds and mention some of their drawbacks. Popular doesn't necessarily mean that breed of dog is for you or your children.

Golden Retrievers

It's no accident that we see lots of cars carrying both children and golden retrievers. Fairly large dogs, in the 60 to 70 pound (27–32 kg) range, the goldens are muscular and powerfully built. They're energetic, yet neither nervous nor hyperactive. As their name implies, they were originally intended for hunting; that built-in instinct to retrieve makes them endlessly eager to fetch the ball. The goldens' even temper has made them dogs of choice for special training (see Chapter 4), and they fit well into families. They have a distinctive, graceful coat that does require regular brushing, as well as some stripping for hot weather, but their coat isn't exaggeratedly long, silky, or full, so they're reasonable to groom and don't shed *too* much of themselves in the house.

The golden retriever is truly a multi-purpose dog.

Labrador Retrievers

Close in popularity to goldens, labs, as they're called, are less heavily coated, making them easier to groom. Labs are somewhat more dedicated to hunting than most goldens, so they make good dual-purpose dogs. They have mellow, steady dispositions and are often used as special needs dogs, as in some Seeing Eye programs. They accept training readily, and their readiness to learn makes them good companions to children. Labs are in a similar size range as goldens—50

Nice labs, going about their business.

to 70 pounds (23–32 kg). Be aware that in all breeds females are generally smaller than males.

Irish Setters

These distinctive dogs with their red coats seem to be making a comeback from dark days when they were overbred and turned into neurotic fools. The correct Irish setter is an aristocratic dog that moves like flowing water. The breed standard emphasizes that the dog should have a broad head and be substantial overall. Its personality should be fun-loving, and anyone who has been in the field with a properly bred and trained Irish knows about that personality. Recently I had the privilege of watching a very nice Irish in the obedience ring. Her joy in the obedience work was apparent—punctuated by sharp barks of happiness after she'd completed each exercise.

Like all setters, the Irish demand regular brushing, but their coat should not be exaggeratedly heavy. Also, like all setters, they want to roam—so thorough obedience training, as well as a secure yard, are necessary to keep them safe. These are not dogs especially well-suited to the city, for they thrive on regular long runs in the fields. Too much confinement can result in dogs that must vent their energy somewhere.

English Setters

I have to admit that I am taken by the grace and beauty of the big, coated setters. The English setter has special beauty, I think, with its flecked coat of varied colors. Slightly smaller than the Irish, the English, too, should move gracefully and freely. Perhaps because the English setters have suffered less from popularity than the Irish, my impression of them is that they are somewhat more reserved than their Irish cousins, but they are still sprightly, outgoing dogs.

Least common of the setters, the Gordon is an excellent field dog.

Everything I said about cities, secure yards, and abundant exercise for the Irish goes for the English. These are very rewarding dogs if you have the place for them and like to spend time in the field.

Gordon Setters

Least known and most substantial of the setters is the Gordon, bred originally in the hills of Scotland. The coat is black with tan markings of chestnut or mahogany hue. The colors are clearly defined. These setters are excellent all-purpose dogs—keen hunters, loyal companions, and gentle with children. I have found them the most calm of the setters, but remember they are sporting dogs, with the ranging tendencies and the exercise requirements of all sporting dogs.

Cocker Spaniels

If you want a small, perky, cheerful dog that loves everybody, you might look closely at the cocker spaniel. These dogs are in the 25 to 35 pound (11–16 kg) range, running about 15 inches (38 cm) tall at the shoulder. For several years cockers suffered from too much popularity. People who didn't know much were breeding them like hamsters and paying little attention to what their disposition should be, so for a while we saw a lot of cockers who snapped at sudden movements and piddled on the rug in fear if anyone looked at them sharply. Fortunately, after several years of diminishing popularity, cockers are again being bred by people who

True sporting dogs, the sunny-tempered cocker spaniel is an excellent house pet, too.

know and love them for their excellent, sunny, intelligent temperament. The cocker should be a broad-headed, mellow dog, ready for fun and games, but neither yappy nor snippy. Though cockers can be steady field dogs, they are equally happy as house dogs. Because of their handy size, they can get plenty of exercise chasing balls in a backyard or going on walks, and they're small enough for a child to handle easily. They do need regular brushing and grooming, because they have abundant,

The springer spaniel has always enjoyed a circle of devotees.

silky coats, but a cocker should not have an exaggerated coat.

Springer Spaniels

More substantial and muscular than cockers, the springer has been fortunate in not attracting the wrong level of popularity and hence has remained a steadily favored all-purpose dog by springer fanciers. These dogs have graceful coats, less flowing and extreme than the cocker's. They're upbeat dogs, as are most of the sporting breeds. They also will demand frequent good runs and are great field dogs, be it for hunting or for an outing in the woods or to the lake.

Collies

"The best dog I ever had with my children was my collie," a friend told me recently.

And indeed, the old-style, broad-headed collie with plenty of room for brains was every bit as wonder-

The well-behaved collie can be trained to fetch family members—or dumbbells in an obedience ring.

ful as the "Lassie" series told us it was. Then, like cockers, collies fell into the wrong hands; people who didn't know what they were doing bred them wholesale, and many of them were brainless nitwits. But a properly bred collie is the calm in-charge guardian and companion children's stories are made of. In a size class with goldens, collies weigh 50 to 75 pounds (23–34 kg), though their abundant coats make them appear bigger. They need regular brushing and stripping for hot weather. Collies are calmer than spaniels and retrievers. An only child is not a lonely child with a collie. And if you have several children whose whereabouts you'd like to keep track of, the collie is your dog. My friend had seven children, and her collie would unerringly fetch any one of them.

German Shepherds

I approach this breed with trepidation, for I've known the best and the worst of dogs among German shepherds. Like collies and cockers, they have suffered at times from their own popularity. I find it interesting that Guide Dogs for the Blind, which uses German shepherds, has their own breeding program and is rigorous about their dogs' temperament as well as their physical soundness. When you get a properly bred German shepherd, you can trust your children to it with no qualms.

In choosing a German shepherd pup, look for massiveness. This ought to be a big, heavily boned, powerful dog. Males weigh 75 to 85 pounds (34–39 kg); females run 60 to 70 pounds (27–35 kg). Beware the snipey, slender, weedy-looking German shepherd; many of these are nervous, skittish, undependable dogs that bite out of fear. The proper German shepherd temperament is steady, fearless but not unduly aggressive, and naturally protective of family and territory. It is proof of proper temperament that these dogs have been trained for years as companions to many kinds of people with special needs. Like all the herding breeds, a good German shepherd wants to round up the family and have them all in one place!

Siberian Huskies

These dogs have a 2000-year history of pure breeding, first introduced to the North American continent in Alaska. Bred for their stamina and ability to flourish in frigid climates, huskies were the only means of transportation for Alaskan and Siberian people for centuries. Cherished for their utilitarian qualities, they also became family pets, though perhaps not quite in the sense of "loyal dog dozing by the hearth," for the temperature of most American homes is uncomfortable for the husky. This truly is a dog that needs its own place outdoors to fall back on when civilization as we know it gets too hot to handle. However, as the husky generally was part of a pack in its native home, the solo family pet will need an outdoor shelter to

The properly bred and trained German shepherd is a loving protector.

Like all working dogs, the Siberian husky wants to know what its job is.

21

A pair of smiling Samoyeds.

Samoyeds

Fluffy white dogs with a smile—that describes Samoyeds. Their distinctive dark eyes and dark noses set off their abundant white, cream, or biscuit coats beautifully, and their attitude indicates a real eagerness for everything life may bring them. These are medium-sized dogs, with the males standing 21 to 23 inches (54–59 cm) at the shoulder and the females, as usual, slightly smaller. To the basic, good working-dog temperament they add that eagerness I mentioned, as well as great curiosity and willingness to learn. They are abundantly coated and need regular basic grooming. At a dog show once I met a woman wearing an unusually lovely white sweater. When I remarked on it, she said, "I made it from my dog's hair," gesturing toward the perfectly groomed Samoyed at the end of her leash.

"Now," she continued, "When I wear this sweater, I always know whether my dog is too warm or too cold."

make up for the comfort of other warm canine bodies.

Huskies are active, graceful, strong dogs—a good choice for the family that enjoys energetic outdoor activities.

Praise is the greatest reward for poodles—and all other breeds.

Poodles

There's no smarter dog than a well-bred standard poodle. Though they're fairly tall, they're also slender dogs under all their coat, and very graceful. Poodles who aren't being shown don't have to be clipped in strange patterns; most people I know keep their poodles in what's known as a "puppy clip." Poodles shed much less than most coated dogs do. You'll often see poodles starring in obedience trials, for the poodle loves to learn. They're another breed with a well developed sense of humor, and they love to play. Some retain their ancient hunting instincts and are good water dogs.

I admit a preference for the standard poodle, especially if there are children in the family, for the standard is more rugged and hence more up for fun and games. However, the miniature poodle (over 10 inches [26 cm] and up to 15 inches [38 cm] at the shoulder) is a game little dog, capable of all the proper poodle intelligence and high spirits of its larger relative. Poodles often suffer from too much popularity; people out for a fast buck breed them, and especially among the smaller poodles, there are some really snappy, yappy, neurotic little dogs available. Be sure you get to visit with the dog parents if you're looking for a poodle puppy.

Beagles

Sturdy, cheerful little dogs, beagles still have their hunting instincts intact, so the child who wants to play endless games of "find the ball" or "retrieve the stick" will have a devoted playmate in a beagle. I've found beagles more home-loving and less likely to take off on a trail than many other hounds, and hence a better choice as a family pet. They do have lovely hound voices, and an unhappy beagle yodeling its grief is unwelcome in an apartment building or a built-up

Beagles have lovely hound voices and enjoy showing them off.

neighborhood. It's unwise to encourage unnecessary howling in a beagle pup. Other than that, beagles present few training or upkeep problems. Smooth-coated, they're good house dogs as long as they have plenty of people who want to take them outside for playtime.

Schipperkes

These are distinctive little black dogs with great flair. They are often pictured at the bow of barges on canals in Belgium and the Netherlands, so many people think of them as the barge dogs and translate their name to mean "little captain." Actually, they were favorite companion dogs in the Low Countries for many centuries. One of its outstanding traits is great curiosity, which makes the Schipperke outstanding as an alarm dog. Added to this alertness is great devotion to the family and an active willingness to defend that family. Schipperkes are gentle with children, yet tough enough to make good playmates. They're smart, outgoing with their family, and reserved towards people they don't know. I think Schipperkes haven't had the popularity they deserve in the United States.

Dachshunds

Roger Caras calls these "animated peapods," which I find a perfect description of the happy, busy little dachshunds. They come in three varieties and two sizes. The varieties are based on coat—smooth; long-haired, with silky coats; and wire-haired, with the rough coat of most terriers. The sizes are basically standard and miniature, though if you get hooked on dachshunds and decide to show them, you'll learn the detailed standards for each size variation. Small they may be, but make no mistake: dachshunds are all dog, and fearless. Last year when our two

An alert Pembroke Welsh corgi.

Great Dane girls came into heat, an enterprising little dachshund male not only came calling, he moved right into the pen with our fragrant girls! It took Kent and me hours to discover where he was getting into the pen, as we're not in the habit of considering holes that small to be entry or exit points. The Danish ladies thought he was the cutest thing since jingle balls and immediately made a pet of him. We nicknamed him Video. Kent found a set of dishes small enough for his food and water, and we enjoyed the notion of our dogs having a dog of their own. Eventually his owners, two young girls from down the road, came looking for their lost dog, and Video cheerfully went back home with his overjoyed owners.

Corgis

"The big dog in the small dog suit" is what corgis have been called, and that's an apt description. Bred for herding, corgis have a steadiness one would expect from dogs that were tailored to a certain job. In addition to their herding duties, corgis today are often used as hearing dogs for people who need such help. There are two varieties of corgi. The Pembroke corgi is born tailless, or nearly so. The Cardigan corgi has a long, sweeping tail. Only about 12 inches (31 cm) tall at the shoulder, the corgi is a solid little dog. Its coat is medium long, presenting no great grooming problems. But it is their steady, loving, easygoing disposition that has endeared corgis to me, despite my preference for large dogs. The corgis I have known have been great with children and easy to have around.

Border Terriers

Tough, funny, scrappy, and careful with children, border terriers are great little dogs, delights to everyone old enough to enjoy dogs. Gilda Ratter, the first border terrier I knew, has various acts she goes through to keep her family and appreciative guests laughing. Borders exhibit what I consider the best of terrier temperament. They have the fire and determination that have made terriers beloved for centuries, but they also have that zest for living and joy in human companionship that mark the best of the terriers. Of their attitude toward children, a serious breeder of borders says, "They go out of their way to be careful and gentle with children."

These are small terriers, not much over 12 inches (31 cm) high and under 20 pounds (9 kg) in weight. Their coat is a typical rough, wiry terrier coat, with no big grooming problems. They're devoted to home and family, excellent watchdogs, and, as I've said, full of joy. One consideration: Because they *are* terriers and zealous in their life's work of exterminating vermin, borders can be tricky around kittens, and one would be a fool to consider having hamsters or other rodent-type pets with a resident border terrier.

Boxers

In the medium size category, the sleek-coated boxer with its distinctive pushed-in nose is one of my personal favorites in the dog world. Boxers are truly devoted to their families, great watchdogs, basically calm in temperament as most working dogs are, but with a keen sense of humor that I value in a dog. Next to Danes, boxers are the silliest dogs I know, yet like Danes, they have the steadiness and dependability that make a good family dog. They use their front paws in an idiosyncratic way that is very like boxing, but like most working dogs, they don't generally play roughly with children too small for the game. They're usually easy to train and easy to keep in the house. The one problem with boxers, like all the brachycephalic (pushed-in-nosed) dogs, is difficulty breathing in very hot weather. One has to be very smart about not leaving a boxer in a car, for it will suffer even more than most dogs when the car heats up.

Border terriers are a delight to young and old alike.

Great Danes

Yes, I am prejudiced. Great Danes have shared my life for the past 28 years, and I've never found them lacking in anything. But more to the point, I've seen and heard such fine stories about Great Danes as excellent nannies/baby-sitters/playmates that I know they're wonderful children's dogs.

DJ, our first adult male Dane, came to us as a six-and-a-half-year-old who had already raised four human children at least to their teen years. To DJ, a child was a responsibility. Its well-being was his business. So I should have been prepared during his first week with us when I took him to visit a friend with small children. The children were playing upstairs, and their squabbling escalated beyond what their mother would tolerate. She marched upstairs, and the next sound I heard was a loud smack, followed by a child's wail.

"Enforcing peace," I thought, readying myself for a quiet continuation of our visit.

But the second wail brought instant response from DJ, who got up from lying at my feet and dashed up the stairs.

My realization kicked in fast, and I was on his tail, tackling him before he made it to the top. I marched him back downstairs and put his leash on him. When my friend reappeared and asked what all the racket had been about, I gave her some Dane wisdom:

"The next time you have to smack the kids, let me know first. DJ doesn't hold with spanking children, and he was on his way to defend them."

DJ's behavior, more or less, is standard Dane reaction to what they perceive as threats to their children. Toddlers get returned unceremoniously to their boundaries by protective Danes. Neighborhood bullies get their comeuppance if they hit a Dane's child, and intruders feel the wrath of a very large, very serious dog. In fact, because of their protective nature, a Dane must be trained early and limits have to be enforced. For that reason, among others, Danes are not for everyone.

Danes are very large dogs—males can weigh close to 200 pounds (91 kg). Not everyone wants to share as much of their living space as a Dane needs. It's not a matter of their needing a lot of exercise; compared to many of the sporting dogs, Danes are couch potatoes. But when you have a resident Dane, you just have a lot of dog around, and a Dane wants nothing quite as much as being close to you. Further, like all the giant breeds, an out-of-hand Dane is a real danger, so you must begin obedience and other training before six months, or you have a most strenuous job on your hands. By nature Danes are cooperative, gentle to their people, and absolutely silly. It is that silliness that makes training tricky, for a Dane will know quickly what makes you laugh, and heaven help you when your 160-pound adult Dane pulls a stunt that you thought was funny when it was a puppy!

Their smooth coat makes grooming Danes very easy, and they're good house dogs because they shed so little. Unfortunately, their giant size contributes to a relatively short life span—9 to 11 years—as is true of all the giant breeds, such as Saint Bernards, Newfoundlands, and Great Pyrenees.

Saint Bernards

My own first experience with Saint Bernards came at an autumn benched dog show many years ago. I was maybe four years old, tired of the long show day, bored, and chilly. My wanderings had brought me to a large bench space occupied by several Saint Bernards. They looked invitingly warm and welcomed me as I climbed up onto the bench and burrowed in among them. It was easy to fall asleep, and hours later, when I emerged from under my fur pile, I was surprised to be greeted by the words, "It's the little lost girl!" I was pretty indignant—I wasn't lost at all, and I'd been in excellent company.

Well-bred Saints are just great children's dogs, though they present all the size problems Danes do, plus more coat to deal with. Like puppies of all the giant breeds, Saint pups are incredibly clumsy. You do *not* want a toddler and a six-month-old Saint at the same

time. The certainties of tumbles, spills, and things knocked over are too great. But an adult Saint is a fine guardian for children.

Newfoundlands

Who can forget the wonderful dog in Peter Pan? Nana was a Newfoundland, and these dogs, members of the working dog group, show the calm, even temperament and the steadfast protectiveness of their families that all working dogs should display. "Newfies" are big, hairy dogs whose very appearance makes you feel they have everything under control. Yet their teddy-bear look belies their staunch defense of their people and their territory. They are gentle with children, but they also enjoy romping with older children and are often avid water dogs. If, like me, you're biased toward big dogs, look at the Newfie. It's a breed that hasn't been blighted by excessive popularity, so you're not likely to find Newfies that have been misbred.

The Newfoundland gives the impression of being in complete, calm control.

* * *

This isn't an exhaustive list, by any means. With close to 150 breeds recognized by the American Kennel Club in the United States alone, you would need to go to a dog encyclopedia to bone up on all the breeds. What I've given here is a sampler of dogs that I know have proved themselves good children's dogs—and, of course, we're talking about humane, reasonable children old enough to respect, love, and cherish dogs. It's possible that any match of the right child and the right dog will work out, but there are minefields of possible problems when you try to pair up a child with a dog of a breed not known for its love of children. Since there are so many, many breeds of dogs, why look for trouble? Of the myriad dog problems I've known about, 95 percent have been people problems—not dog problems—the wrong dog with the wrong people. That's why our animal shelters bulge with abandoned, unwanted dogs and our roadsides are marked by the corpses of dogs who never got a chance at the right home.

A Dog for Older Relatives

Some of the traits I consider for a dog intended primarily for people 60 or older include easy upkeep, cheerful disposition, funny, loyal, and easily amused. I've been taking note of the dogs that older people have with them in campgrounds; many of these are small dogs. Now partly this may be a camper space limitation, but also, many older people are choosing to live in smaller homes, so it's not only people who go about in RVs that choose smaller dogs. I've also noticed how quiet and well-behaved these dogs are. You just don't hear yapping dogs in camp. Probably the major criterion for older people is that the dog will enhance its people's lives. So if you're considering a canine gift for an older person, don't, for instance, get a saluki for a person who gets tired going through the supermarket, or a Saint Bernard for someone who has just recovered from a broken hip!

Poodles

I've discussed the standard and the miniature poodles earlier, and either would fit here, too, but I want to add the toy poodle. Under 10 inches (26 cm) in height, these tiny fluffballs are still all poodle—smart, funny, eager to frisk around an apartment chasing their toys, and great watchdogs. They're nice lap companions and can have all the sterling characteristics of their larger relatives. All poodles have been somewhat overbred, seen by people who neither know nor care about the standard for the breed as the ticket to a fast buck. But the smaller poodles have, I think, suffered more because they appear to be easier to keep than their larger cousins. Thus, when choosing a

miniature, be careful to get to know the dog's parents and check out their dispositions. Poodles were never meant to be snappish, neurotic, sickly things, and you don't want one of those, nor do you want to foist one off on an older friend.

Yorkshire Terriers

With their silky, flowing coats and quick pitter-pattering gait, Yorkies look to me like heavily coated bugs dancing along. They are curious about everything, alert, happy little dogs that seem to be just in love with life. These are dogs that can do very well in small apartments or condos and get their exercise mostly indoors, yet I see many of them also eagerly scoping out their surroundings in woodsy campgrounds. They're true terriers—quick, smart, aggressive, and fine for warning that strangers approach.

Miniature Schnauzers

Here's another little charmer—from 12 to 14 inches (31–36 cm) high—that likes nothing more than to spend its days amusing its owner. Schnauzers have the typical terrier exuberance, which makes them playmates, clowns, and floor shows all rolled into one. Terriers in general are busy, bouncy dogs. You love the terrier temperament or you can't stand it. Schnauzers are excellent warning dogs, though like all terriers they need to be taught when to be quiet. They should be neither shy nor vicious. They have wiry coats that need some grooming, but they're not rampant shedders and make good house dogs.

Smooth Fox Terriers

These dogs used to be very popular, and they deserve a look, especially for an older person. Their former favor was based, I think, on

Yorkshires want to know everything that's going on.

Miniature schnauzers are good warning dogs.

29

their absolute loyalty to their owners. I remember them as steadier than many of the more racy terriers. One of my friends had a smooth fox terrier that he took hunting, and that was one tough, gutsy little dog. He was also an excellent watchdog.

The smooth fox terrier is about 15 inches (38 cm) at the shoulder, weighing around 18 pounds (8 kg). Its smooth coat makes it a fine house dog with no grooming problem; its optimistic temperament makes the smooth fox terrier eager to go wherever its owner goes.

Boston Terriers

Here's another dog that used to enjoy greater popularity than it has seen lately. Perhaps its eclipse was due to injudicious breeding, as has been true of so many popular breeds. Generally the Boston is a dog for one or two people, making it ideal for the older folks with no children around. Smooth-coated, Bostons weigh from 15 to 25 pounds (7–11 kg), with most being in the smaller range, making them nice lap size. Like other brachycephalic dogs, Bostons sometimes have breathing problems, especially in extreme heat. They can live very nicely, thank you, in an air-conditioned house or apartment, and will willingly forego tiring romps in the fields.

Scottish Terriers

Short, muscular, dignified little dogs, Scotties have all the aggressiveness we associate with terriers. They're devoted to their people, but not especially dependable with children, so I'd recommend Scotties for older people not likely to have active children around. With typical wiry terrier coats, Scotties are easy to groom. They're also fun to have around, eager to chase and retrieve balls and other toys.

Pekingese

These abundantly coated little dogs were originally bred, we are told, to warm the sleeves of the nobility in their castles in China. Small they may be, but Pekingese deserve their nickname of "Lion Dog of China." Here we have another dog that can live very well with little more exercise than an apartment or a small yard offers; a companion dog *par excellence.*

The Scottie may look dignified, but it's all terrier.

Pomeranians

The official breed standard for the Pomeranian says, "a compact, short-coupled dog, well-knit in frame. (He) should exhibit great intelligence in expression, docility in disposition, and activity and buoyancy in deportment..." In the Pom, you're looking at a bundle of dog in a 4 to 5 pound (1.8–2.3 kg) package adorned in a distinctive, puffy coat. Poms fit well into apartments or small homes and are excellent companions for older folks. Their size makes them not especially well-suited to small children. They sound the alarm readily, and, if anything, need to be taught when to be quiet!

Lhasa Apsos

If you're looking for a little dog with a lot of presence and personality, the Lhasa is a good candidate. Under 1 foot (31 cm) tall at the shoulder and densely coated, Lhasas are assertive and cheerful with their families. They are not immediately friendly with strangers, which makes them good at sounding the alarm when strangers are around. Busy little dogs, they can get enough exercise playing in a house or apartment, but they are sturdy enough to enjoy a good walk. Without being overly intrusive, the Lhasa demands a good deal of attention from its owner, making it an ideal dog for a person who wants lots of companionship.

Shi Tzus

Also known as the Lion Dog, the Shih Tzu is an extremely coura-

A puffy little Pomeranian being groomed.

geous little dog, and therein may lie one of its drawbacks. It must be taught not to challenge big dogs. Less than a foot tall at the shoulders, the Shih Tzu is a densely-coated little dog, with a shaggy, coarse texture that needs regular attention to grooming. It is thought that the Shih Tzu is a cross between the Lhasa Apso and the Pekingese. Its personality is much more dominant than the Lhasa's; for this reason, it takes a stronger training hand than either of its forebears. I wouldn't recommend the Shih Tzu for either a timid person or

There's a lot of determination beneath the Shi Tsu's cute exterior.

a family with small children; but for a person ripe for a challenge, this is a nice choice.

Shetland Sheepdogs

The Sheltie looks like a little collie. It should be no more than 16 inches (41 cm) at the shoulder. Bred to herd sheep, the Sheltie should have that

The Sheltie, developed to herd sheep, makes an excellent family pet.

steadiness we associate with dogs of the herding breeds. This is a perky little dog, yet good for older people, for though Shelties need their daily walk, their pace fits well with an older person. Because of my bias toward the working and herding breeds and their calm temperament, I prefer a well-bred Sheltie to any terrier for day-to-day livability.

Weimaraners

For the hunter who still wants to spend time in the field, no dog beats the Weimaraner. Covered with a sleek, short coat, 25 to 27 inches (64–69 cm) at the shoulder, this glorious dog has forgotten more about hunting than most people ever know. When a Weimaraner gets done quartering a field and says there is no game in it, you can take that to the bank. Weimies don't win often at field trials because they're so thorough; faster, flashier dogs have run the course and gone to the finish line while the Gray Ghost is still checking every bush and thicket. But for those who don't view a day in the field as a time when they have to set speed records, this is the dog. I had my best hunting team in Bucky, a Weimaraner, and Sapphire, a Dane. Bucky found and pointed the birds beautifully. Sapphire got bored with his point and would burst into the cover, starting the bird. As it flew up, she'd leap, grab it, break its neck, and retrieve it to my hand. Meanwhile, Bucky looked for another bird.

Weimaraners are brilliant dogs, and they are dogs that truly suffer when separated from their people, making them ideal dogs for retired folks who can spend lots of time with their canine. Do check that the breeder from whom you're getting a Weimaraner sticks closely to the breed standard, though; some breeders have produced a high-strung dog that does not show correct temperament.

Cocker Spaniels, Dachshunds, and Corgis

I listed these earlier as good choices for children's dogs, and they also fit well for older people. (For cocker spaniels, see page 19; for dachshunds, see page 24; for corgis, see page 24.)

* * *

Again, this is by no means a complete list, and it's colored by my own biases. I have known nice Chihuahuas, and many older folks are devoted to theirs. The pug is another dog many people cherish. Just don't foist off more dog than an older person can handle. Or, if you happen to be the older person, try to remember that you're probably not as limber as you were the last time you began to civilize your favorite breed of puppy. Ask yourself: Am I really up to that again?

A Dog for You, Yourself

Afghans

Ah, with only yourself to please, what wide horizons the world of dogs offers! Without the worry of having a child heedlessly leave a gate open as an escape hatch, you can consider living with a lovely, aloof Afghan hound, who, running loose, could cover half the county in an afternoon. The Afghan will reward you with an occasional nod of recognition if you are faithful and keep a good kitchen, and no dog— just regally lying around—will do more to upgrade the decor of your house.

Chow Chows

With no one else to consider, you can spend your life with a chow who will give you absolute devotion in return. Though chows can be

Regal Afghans can put on bursts of speed up to 60 mph when pursuing game.

integrated into families, they give their real love to only one person in that family and present interesting challenges to the big family that expects a dog to share affection with everyone equally. My friend Ken has a chow, Oso, who truly does not bother to recognize any other human being. When Ken leaves Oso with us, the dog sometimes deigns to respond to my husband's voice, but me Oso totally ignores.

There's only one problem with having a dog that bonds solely with one person—what happens if another person is added? Some one-person dogs will tolerate another person, though the newcomer ought not to expect any particular love or attention from the dog. Indeed, if you plan to bond a dog solely to you, you need to give some thought to what will happen should you become ill or have to kennel your companion. I believe that all dogs should be socialized to the point of recognizing people in general as tolerable and deserving of respect. Veterinarians must be able to treat any dog without the threat of being mauled. Many years ago there were a lot of hair-trigger-tempered Dobermans, unpredictably nasty. After too many bad episodes, veterinarians let it be known that unless breeders could find a way to produce better-tempered Dobermans, veterinarians were going to find it in their hearts to refuse to treat the nasty ones. Today we find much nicer dobies than we saw thirty years or so ago.

No Attack Dogs

Rottweilers

There's a pernicious tendency right now to breed certain large dogs to be overaggressive. I think at once of rottweilers. These are working dogs, supposed to be staunch, even-tempered family dogs with work to do. Before their current wave of popularity, the rottweilers I knew were exactly what one expects of working dogs—calm, steady, dependable, even-tempered dogs, much like Danes but without the Dane silliness. Then someone decided rottweilers were ideal dogs to scare other people with, and experimenters began using high-strung specimens for breeding

Rottweilers should be steady, mellow companion dogs.

stock. Because all breeds of dogs are basically humanly engineered constructs, any breed can be bent to the pattern people decide is ideal. Many fine dogs have been so changed by human ideas of what they ought to be that their original breeders wouldn't recognize them today. Once not very long ago, few rottweilers existed. The people who bred and owned them valued them for their original characteristics.

This is not to condemn all rottweilers, please understand. Even from aggressive parents, a rottweiler puppy, taught carefully and impressed that people are to be loved, not bitten, can grow up to be the good, steady dog it was intended originally to be. But one would be better off getting a pup from parents of steady temper.

Akitas

Another large dog that is being improperly billed is the Akita. Akitas, too, are working dogs, with all that implies about calm temperament. Like all working dogs, the Akita protects its family, but it wasn't designed to go looking for trouble.

The fault lies in people's mistaken ideas about what a personal dog is. Yes, truly I have always known that I am safe wherever I go with one of my Danes, but *not* because any of my Danes has ever been trained as an attack dog. Quite the contrary. I teach a puppy that the human hand is not a toy, not to be gnawed on, nor is any other human appendage. But no one should raise a hand in anger to the owner of a Dane and expect to take that hand back unscathed. That's simply the nature of the Dane—and of the Doberman, and the rottweiler, and the Akita, and the German shepherd—and we could go on through the entire working class of dogs. So if you're looking for a personal dog that will love and protect you, you need to choose the breed that's right for you and then take that puppy into your home and your heart. Train it to be a good citizen. Socialize it to know people as friends. Every dog knows friend from foe—instinctively. Forget the attack training; very few people are dominant enough to live with an attack-trained dog. Even fewer people, I suspect, have so many enemies that they need an attack trained dog!

Other Interesting Dogs

Though not all of the dogs I'm going to mention here are one-person dogs, because many of them are complex and flourish under a lot of attention, they qualify as dogs you might be more likely to consider for yourself than for a family.

Dalmatians

Moving up rapidly in popularity right now, the "coach dog," with its distinctive spotted coat, is one of the complex dogs. Dalmatians can

The striking color pattern of Dalmatians does not breed true.

Airedale Terriers

These big terriers run upwards of 23 inches (59 cm) at the shoulders and are muscular. My friend David has a female Airedale tough enough to run down, kill, and haul home wild pigs, which gives you some idea of what these dogs can be. Airedales demand attention from their owners and have an active sense of mischief and fun. They tend to be aggressive with other dogs and are very territorial. They have an enthusiastic cadre of fanciers, for they're complex, interesting dogs.

be stubborn, wanting to go their way. Rambunctious as puppies, they're a poor choice for young children or older, frail people, as they do not make any accommodations for either. Yet they're devoted to their owners, alternating periods of intense activity with long periods of quiet. Correct color does not breed true in dalmatians, so the striking spotting that is correct does not show up in all puppies in a litter.

Doberman Pinschers

These sleek, classy dogs don't deserve their bad reputation any longer, as I've said. Because of their extreme intelligence and their tendency to bond primarily to one person, they're a wonderful choice for the one-or-two-person family. Properly, Dobermans have a fiery but predictable disposition. They do wonderfully in obedience work, and flourish even more than most dogs when constantly challenged to learn something new.

Alaskan Malamutes

If you want a dog that isn't always needy for attention, the mals are for you. Here's a dog that can truly keep itself amused for hours without your intervention. Malamutes flourish in packs, dislike the heat of most houses, and live to pull sleds. I know of no more stirring sight than watching friends hook up

Airedale terriers are special dogs and a joy to people who are up to them.

"barkless," basenjis are not, as I once thought, silent. They scream. They yodel. And they scheme. Mostly they scheme about how to escape any enclosure their owners have dared to devise. The subplot to all their schemes is to be around their owners and busy doing what they want to do. Conveniently medium in size, smooth-coated, the basenjis, because of their high intelligence, need a lot of their owner's attention.

Borzois

Also known as Russian wolfhounds, borzois are elegance personified. With their streamlined build and curling coat, they are a joy to look at. A friend had a young borzoi to whom she had given a very elegant name, for she was training him for an elegant dog show career. I found that he answered happily to Rosco, a shortened version of his name, and appreciated my throwing sticks for him to retrieve. He was

their 12-dog malamute team to the sled. Quivering with anticipation, the dogs take their places on the string, barely able to stand the wait until the last dog is in harness, the driver is on the sled, and they hear the command to *Go.* As one, they leap into the pull, yelping their joy at being on the road again!

Obviously, we're not talking about your average, lie-about suburban dog here. Getting a malamute—or, more likely, malamutes—implies that you're going to get involved with the kind of work these dogs are bred for. This is an excellent example of choosing the right dog for the situation, not trying to bend the dog into something it isn't.

Basenjis

When dog fanciers get together to swap war stories, the two groups that have the most curdling tales of brilliant dogs driving their owners up the wall are the Weimaraner owners and the basenji owners. Touted as

Borzois personify elegance.

robust, tough, playful, and not at all the dandified dog she made him out to be. His story makes me wonder again at how much we turn our dogs into our idea of what they're supposed to be instead of what they would be naturally.

Italian Greyhounds

If I wanted a little, clean dog to carry around and laugh at, I might well choose an Italian greyhound. Many weigh less than 8 pounds (3.6 kg), and they stand perhaps 14 inches (36 cm) at the shoulder. Their coat is so short and sleek that when I held my first Italian greyhound, I felt as if I were holding a baby bird before it had feathered out. The I.G.s I've known have been relatively flighty, curious, and friendly. Contortionists all, they amuse me with their postures, and their big eyes give them a perpetually amazed expression. I definitely wouldn't suggest an I.G. around children, for they are delicate, fine-boned dogs.

How Do I Learn More?

One of the best ways to dog-shop is to visit a benched dog show. Every region of the United States has its prestigious benched show, often two-day affairs when all the dogs must be present and in their places for most of each day. Here you can see more breeds of dog than you imagined exist, talk with their owners, and often meet some of the most serious dog breeders. You will, of course, be talking with people who are absolutely convinced that their breed is the best. Often, though, the serious breeder will tell you why you don't want that kind of dog, for people committed to a breed don't want any of their chosen dogs where either the dogs or the people will be unhappy with the match. If you persist once you find the breed that wins your heart, you'll learn all you'll ever need to know and more. Much as I value books, I find a dog show the best place to soak in dogs, size them up, and pick the brains of people who have experienced the dogs I'm interested in. Later I'll deal with how you actually decide from whom to buy your dog.

No Wrong Breeds

I want to stress again that the smorgasbord of dog breeds gives every one of us the chance to get exactly the right dog for our circumstances. Every breed has its own enthusiastic following. The more you steep yourself in every aspect of the breeds you're considering, narrowing and narrowing the choices until you select one, the better is your chance of making a doggy match you'll live with long and happily.

The unquestionably wrong choice is the impulse buy, thinking, "If I don't like this dog, I can take it to the pound."

Chapter 3
Where Shall I Get My Puppy?

Now matters get dicey. You're settled on what kind of puppy or dog you want. Where is your canine companion for the next decade or more going to come from? It is nearly as important to get the dog from the right people as it is to get the right dog. If, indeed, you're getting a purebred puppy, the breeder from whom you get it has made several vital decisions already. Issues of heredity, prenatal health, and early development are already set. If you've decided to skip the puppy stages and get an adult dog, its present owners have shaped its attitude toward people, as well as toward other animals.

There are four basic sources where people get dogs or puppies:
1. Longtime or professional breeders
2. "Backyard" breeders
3. Animal shelters
4. Special-purpose dog organizations

Let's look at each source in detail, and I'll arm you with some questions to ask and some physical aspects to be aware of. In this chapter I'll deal with numbers 1 and 2. The others will be in the next chapter.

Important Warnings

Before we mush on, a couple of warnings are warranted. First, don't let sympathy sway you to acquire a pet. When I volunteered at the humane society shelter, Kent was terrified every week that I'd come home with a whole entourage of puppies, kittens, and dogs that had tugged successfully at my heartstrings. As a matter of fact, although I used every contact I had among animal lovers to place many pets, I actually rescued only one dog myself, a Great Dane who had been caught in a leg trap for weeks and weighed perhaps 50 pounds (23 kg) when Kent carried her out of the shelter. There was a calico cat named Patches I worked extra hard to find a good home for, because she was special and I wanted her. There was also a strange springer spaniel who pasted himself to the

When visiting a kennel, make sure that the puppies' accommodations are roomy and clean.

always get homes of a sort if they're packaged with just the right photogenic child at just the right time. Having done all your research on what puppy you want and why, don't let impulse tempt you. True, you might get lucky, but you're just as likely to stick yourself with a dog that you really don't like all that much and that you feel guilty about. The dogs that crowd the animal shelters were all someone's bad choice.

Now, let's look at some sources for your puppy.

cage door and claimed he had been born to be my dog, though he was relatively unfriendly to most other people, and I exerted a lot of effort to find him the right home. Being realistic, I knew that Kent and I already had all the cats and dogs we could properly care for. Adding more out of sympathy would have meant that none of the animals would have had enough. Further, I would have been setting up for potential dog and cat fights and creating an all-round bad situation. I had the pets I could care for. My heart hurt for the ones I couldn't place, but Kent and I are a family, not an animal refuge.

Just as dangerous as sympathy is impulse. Until she got her cats spayed, one of my friends sent her pretty little blonde daughter to the shopping mall regularly with boxes of cute kittens. It was an advertiser's dream package, and the "free" kittens always went somewhere, just as the "free" puppies, too,

Longtime or Professional Breeders

One good way to locate a longtime breeder is by phoning or writing the American Kennel Club (see Other Resources section page 91) and asking for the contact person in say, the Standard Schnauzer Club of America. You'll most likely be put in touch with the secretary of that group, who will have a list of breeders to whom you'll be referred. This method will lead you to folks who show their dogs a lot, are serious about their chosen breed, and who have joined the national or regional club.

Another way to find serious breeders is by answering ads in one of the national dog magazines—*Dog World,* for instance. Although many breed clubs have their own specialty magazines, most of these aren't available on newsstands. Further, many of them are devoted more to bragging about recent show wins than they are to selling puppies. Newspaper ads, too, can lead you to serious breeders.

How am I defining this group? What sets them apart? Probably first, they truly live for their chosen breeds. If asked, many will honestly tell you that they've seldom made money on their dogs. They don't have puppies all the time, for they care for their females and don't wear them out producing litter after litter. They know their breed standard and breed to it, not to the current fad in the breed. They undoubtedly do some showing, but many of them spend most of their money on good care and quarters for their dogs. They have dogs of all ages in their home and kennels, for they are committed to every dog they choose to keep and don't turn the oldsters out when their breeding days are done. Most of them prefer that their chosen breed not become wildly popular, for with poularity comes an explosion in the numbers of people breeding those dogs, generally with little regard for what the breed should be and even less regard for the kinds of homes the puppies get. They will ask you rude questions in an attempt to discover whether you are really up for that particular kind of dog. Even if they do have puppies, they may tell you to go home and think over your possible acquisition of a pup, making sure that's what you want.

Let me tell you about a boxer breeder I'll never forget, and you'll see what I mean. She was in her fifties, a plain little woman in sensible shoes and jeans. I'll call her Mary. She worked the night shift in a nearby factory to support herself and her dogs, whom she kenneled in a large, clean barn with attached pens. Two members of my family went to see Mary and her boxers in response to her ad in a regional newspaper. First she sat us down in her rather bare living room to quiz us on what we knew about boxers. As we'd studied the breed thoroughly, we passed that part handily. Mary then let the father of the puppies in from another room so we could see him and, I think, to observe us with the dog.

"Brutus doesn't really like puppies all that much," Mary told us,

The Anatolian shepherd is relatively new in North America.

"so I'll let him go back to his bedroom while I bring in a couple of the puppies."

Back she came shortly, a sleek puppy under each arm. Those pups gleamed with good health, and they took over the room with a sureness that told me that this was hardly their first time inside.

"May we go out and see the rest of the pups?" I asked.

"No. Not yet. I want you to have a chance to see each puppy and get to know them apart. The whole litter (there were eight) will only confuse you at this point."

So we spent a very long afternoon with pairs of puppies. Then Mary brought in only their mother, having warned us that Gretchen was thin and out of coat. Gretchen was surely not ready to step inside a show ring the next day, but for a mother who'd brought up the tribe we had just seen, she was in remarkably good condition. With Gretchen sprawled on a couch, we next pored over puppy pedigrees. Not only was Mary raising a splendidly healthy litter of outgoing pups, she had studied boxers and put together probably the best lineage I've ever seen on one pedigree. Nor were the boxers on that pedigree just names on a piece of paper. Mary knew or knew about each ancestor for five generations back and could tell us not only their wins, but, more importantly, their dispositions and general health and soundness. It was a seminar on great boxers.

Finally we trekked out to the barn, Mary in the lead carrying a huge pan of food for the pups. There, in clean, good-smelling straw, the eight puppies romped, interrupting immediately to dive into their supper. By this time we could tell one from the others, and were settling on a feisty little bitch. However, we were not to take her home with us that day.

"Go home and think about it," Mary instructed us. "Be sure she's the one you want."

"Can we put a deposit on her?" we wanted to know.

"No. I won't be selling her tomorrow. You give me a call one way or the other." Darkness was drawing down, and Mary looked at her watch. "I've got to clean up here now and get ready for work."

Well, of course we got the little bitch, whom we named Gay, plus a list of do's and don'ts a mile long, plus her pedigree and health records. I now know I was right when I thought I saw tears glittering in Mary's eyes as we closed the car door and drove away, because I've always cried when one of our dogs left, too. To me, Mary stands out as the epitome of the serious dog breeder. She phoned us to make sure all was well, and we knew she was available should we have any questions about Gay. Mary lived for her boxers, bred them well and sparingly, placed then carefully in loving homes, and was a credit to her calling. Yes, we paid top dollar for Gay, and she was worth every penny of it.

Watch Out For . . .

- The breeders who have several breeds, especially if all of those are the currently most popular dogs. That's a sign that the people are in it mostly for the money, not the care and well-being of purebred dogs.
- Breeders who don't know what weaknesses and faults their chosen breed is prone to. It was from a conscientious collie breeder that I learned of PRA, progressive retinal atrophy. Jean had just come from the vet's where—sadly but responsibly—she had had an entire litter put down. This litter of great promise, when their eyes were tested, turned out to be a fatally flawed litter.
- Breeders who don't have old dogs around. This is a sign that these are what we call "puppy mills." All they're interested in is litter after litter of puppies.
- Any breeder who hedges on the subject of a dog's pedigree and registration. If both parents are registered with the AKC (American Kennel Club), then registering the litter is a simple matter. If both parents aren't registered, a warning should sound in your mind— why not? How can anyone produce sound dogs of any breed without knowing the exact background of both parents?

- Any breeder that is going to charge you extra for registering the puppy or for providing the proper AKC registration form plus a valid, five-generation pedigree. True, you may not be planning to show or breed your pet, but the AKC says flatly that registration papers shall not be a matter of extra cost to the puppy buyer. Peddling the paperwork is sleazy.
- Any breeder who won't let you see either parent. What's wrong with the parents? Why should you want one of their pups?
- Any breeder who won't let you see where the puppy has been living. It's true that puppies are remarkably messy en masse, but all of us can tell the difference between today's mess and a buildup of uncleaned pens or filthy sleeping quarters.
- Breeders who don't have any of the dogs they claim to value living with them. True, a few breeds like malamutes prefer the yard to the house, but most people who really love their dogs have them in the house, at least some of the time.
- Breeders who overstate their dogs' possibilities. Yes, a man I know guaranteed that in five years one of his Irish setter puppies would finish its championship or he'd refund the purchaser's money. But that was a special case. The purchaser had been hounding Irish setter breeders for several years, insisting

that each ought to be able to guarantee that whatever pup they sold him would finish a championship. He was an unrealistic person and a genuine pain. My friend put a stiff price on the puppy in question, knowing that one of two things would happen. Either the man would turn the offer down (he did!), or he'd take such stellar care of the dog and hire such an outstanding show handler that the dog would finish. No one can tell exactly how a puppy will come out. Further, we can't tell what kind of care even a seemingly dedicated purchaser will give the pup. So guaranteeing a future champion is balderdash.

- Arrogant breeders. Serious breeders may seem rude in some of their questions as they try to qualify you as a serious prospect for a dog of their breed, yet underlying all the questions, you can see the concern. But there are some breeders who act as if the world should genuflect as they pass and who treat all questioners as impudent peasants. Pass such people up. You don't need to abase yourself to get a nice dog.

Backyard Breeders

These are the folks who may live down the street from you, or who advertise their puppies in a local paper. The major difference between the backyard breeders (hereafter referred to as BBs) and the professional is scale. They often have one excellent female, have studied the breed, and know that she has sound qualities that deserve to be passed on. Many pros began as backyard breeders. Generally, BBs have the puppies' mother as their personal pet. Often they have many pictures of the father, for he is likely to be an outstanding example of his breed. You'll often find the puppies in a spare bedroom or having taken over the family room. When I say "having taken over," I immediately think of the two fine young people in Oregon who bred their black bitch to our blue Dane, Killer. She had, heaven help us all, sixteen puppies! Jean and Jerry had set up her whelping box in a corner of their study. When I went to visit the seven-week-old puppies, I arrived at feeding time. Jean and Jerry had a couple of helpers, and all four paraded past me into the study with restaurant-sized trays of puppy food.

Two-week-old yellow Lab puppies.

"Puppy, puppy, puppy," called Jean, waking them. From an alcove in the room came more Dane puppies than I had ever seen before at one place and time. It was a tidal wave of black and blue puppies, washing over the food trays and licking them clean in moments.

Those two people had done everything humanly possible to bring their puppy mob along well and spare the mother as much as they could. They took separate lunch hours. Jean might be first, and she'd bottle-feed the eight blue pups. Then Jerry would come home and bottle-feed the eight black ones, thus relieving the mother of one feeding a day. They began weaning the pups early, letting the mother feed them when she wanted to, but making sure the pups didn't need Mom all that much. Because they knew they wanted to keep only one pup and chose it early, they lined up prospective homes for the rest, taking deposits to ensure seriousness in the prospects. They kept all the pups with the litter until the end of their eighth week, which is the optimum time to send them to their new homes; although they were overwhelmed with puppies, they were picky about whom they sold pups to. Financially, they may have broken even on the litter, although profit wasn't their chief motive for breeding their bitch.

Both humans were exhausted when the puppy episode was over, and they decided not to breed their

A two-week-old puppy is tiny and fragile.

female again. But what they did and the care with which they chose the appropriate Dane for their female's partner puts them in that class of backyard breeders I'd gladly get a puppy from.

Jean and Jerry, unfortunately, aren't the only kind of BBs there are. As long as you steel yourself against impulse or sympathy purchases, feel confident in answering puppy ads from BBs. Then let common sense, your eyes, ears, and nose be your guides as to whether you want a puppy from the circumstances you see.

Watch Out For . . .

- Unsanitary living conditions for mother and/or puppies. A litter of puppies that has to be dug out from under a porch or a shed isn't being cared for optimally and obviously hasn't been socialized properly.
- Unthrifty puppies—or a badly out-of-condition mother. The first

few weeks of puppies' lives are as important as those of a human baby. If the litter hasn't had prenatal care and optimum diet and care right after birth, you're looking at future problems. Lack of any veterinary care—no immunizations, for instance—tells you that these puppies are being produced on the cheap.

- People who know little or nothing about their chosen breed. If your studies have already put you ahead of the people who have the pup you're considering, you might be wise to look elsewhere. Since all current breeds of pure-bred dogs are human constructs, all also have their faults. A knowledgeable breeder knows these and tries to avoid them. I wonder how a woman I saw at a Dane specialty show feels about the person who sold her Dane to her. Totally ignorant of Dane color standards, she arrived ringside with a white Dane splotched with brindle patches. You could always tell where she was by the swiveling heads and craning necks of all the other Dane owners present!

- Besides dumb, blind ignorance, there are con artists in the dog business, just as everywhere else. You *don't want* the "rare, white boxer." Or German shepherd. Or Dane. These dogs are generally deaf, often have sight problems, and even more often have rotten dispositions. Any ad that touts some rare sport of any breed ought not to be your invitation to buy.

- Though you might take a chance on a puppy that's being shoved out of the litter before eight weeks if the breeding is so good you can't pass it up, this borders on a sympathy purchase. It really is important to canine development for puppies to learn to socialize with other dogs, and they learn this in the seventh and eighth weeks with their littermates. Some people are sick of the mess and expense of puppies long before that time and want nothing more than to move them out. Especially if you have other dogs at home, you can work around the socializing aspect. But be aware that you're buying a potential problem.

- Smile, nod at appropriate times, and leave as soon as you can if you meet a BB who tells you that her cousin got a male Swamphound, and since she has a female Swamphound, it just made sense to breed the two of them—they got along so well and all. No, she doesn't know what their pedigrees are; that's not important. But if you really care, she'll try to find out whether either Swamphound is registered with the AKC.

Most permutations of this story tell you that these are accidental puppies. While chance, of course, operates, you might get a good specimen of the breed from such random breedings, but do remember that chance operates negatively, too.

- As with any other source of pure-bred dogs, any iffiness about registrations or pedigrees is a red flag. Ethical breeders know that you're entitled to the puppy's registration form and pedigree. These are more than pieces of paper to them, and they'll maybe even bore you crosseyed with the details of who's who among the ancestors, but this information is worth caring about.

- A wide variation from usual prices for a pup of that breed is a sign that something's going on. A very low price may say, "These puppies are eating us out of house and home, and we want them out of here!" If everything else checks out, you lucked into a bargain. But if other signs point to ignorance, neglect, or abuse, don't get duped. Equally distrust the unusually high price, especially if you're also told some story about how rare these pups are or how sure they are to become world-beaters.

Puppy Mills

Of all the places in the world to get a puppy, a puppy mill is the last one you want to go to. You might do very well consulting the staff of a responsible, local pet store for information about who has puppies for sale. Many breeders get their dog food, leashes, dog toys, and so forth from their local pet store. Most of these pet store owners are animal lovers, many of them active in the local kennel club. They know who in the local dog world is feeding a top diet to their dogs and who's doing it on the cheap, who consults regularly with veterinarians and who's giving their own shots to save a buck. They're like the legendary hairdresser, except that they'll tell.

There is probably no other subject on which dog fanciers agree so fervently as that of puppy mills. I used the term "puppy mill" when I was warning you of things to beware of with professional breeders. The actual puppy mills are concentration camps for dogs. If you've missed seeing any of the periodic television exposés of puppy mills, you probably sleep better than do those of us who haven't. Throughout the country but especially in the Midwest, these hellholes flourish. Dogs are housed—if they're housed at all—in anything handy. Wire cages are common, stacked as high as they'll go, with no protection from urine, feces, or slopped water for the dogs on the lower levels, and often no protection at all from wind, rain, snow, or sun. Many females never get to walk on the green earth and have deformed nails and feet from a lifetime on wire. Flimsy pens, often with several females, their mutual puppies, and perhaps a male or two all in the same enclosure are everyday sights in these slave camps. Food is commonly thrown on the ground, and survival of the fittest is the name of the game. When a female is past breeding age, she's killed, though many females die in puppybirth, since such niceties as prenatal care or veterinarians' attention are not present in these disgraceful testaments to human greed.

Puppies are commonly shipped at four weeks. Some years ago, an activist organization called American Dog Owners' Association did get laws passed that stopped the crowding of puppies into the kind of crate lettuce is packed in; however, puppies are still shipped several to a cage and shipped entirely too early. However, since moving the merchandise is what puppy mills are all about, proper emotional development of puppies is hardly a priority! Who wants to warehouse merchandise that eats?

These puppies, bred in unsanitary conditions and from iffy parentage, are technically purebred dogs. The puppy mill operator generally gets $30 to $45 each for them.

Retailers that sell these puppies also have an imperative to move the merchandise as quickly as possible. The pups are, after all, growing—and eating up the profits. Sickly puppies are kept in back rooms and given minimal health care; after all, the investment isn't high, but taking the pup to a veterinarian would cut the profits. People who have worked at these places tell of the grief they felt mornings when they had to load dead puppies into garbage cans.

The puppies that live are sold for top prices. The pup that was acquired for $35 brings $350 to $500. Yes, the purchasers of these pathetic survivors get all the requisite AKC paperwork. How dependable that paperwork is you may guess at, for the puppy mill where the pup originated is none too fussy about which dog mated with which bitch— or even whose puppies they are.

"And where is the AKC in all this?" you may ask in outrage.

The American Kennel Club is a registering organization, not a policing one. There have been rare cases in which a puppy mill owner has been shut down because of gross irregularities, but these cases occur mainly because some local kennel club gets outraged and makes an airtight case against the puppy miller. It's important to realize that the breeding, care, shipping, and treatment of purebred dogs and cats comes under the authority of the Agriculture Department. Cows and horses and sheep and pigs can stay out in all kinds of weather, eat their food off the ground, and have their young with no human supervision. So what's the big deal about dogs and cats? Before we can have a reasonable authority to appeal to on outlawing puppy mills, we need to get oversight of dogs and cats out of the Agriculture Department.

No doubt I've made my point, and you understand clearly why people who love, value, and spend their lives with dogs despise such businesses as I've described. Since their only motivation is economic, the only way to stop them is to boycott them. When these puppies are not being sold, the puppy mills will wither away.

I had a stunning experience with a puppy mill survivor several years ago. A young couple from Sacramento had carefully chosen their Dane puppy from us, having waited most of a year for us to have a litter available. They had visited and taken pictures from the time the pup's eyes were open, driving five hours each way to see their puppy and his littermates. One Saturday evening they were having dinner with Kent and me, their puppy snoring on the rug in the dining room. There was a knock at the door.

Another young couple from our home town had gone to Sacramento the previous week and bought a Dane puppy—same color, same age as our litter—from an outlet that dealt with puppy mills. Now the puppy wasn't walking, and would we take a look at it?

Soon all four of us were out on the front lawn looking at the most pathetic example of a Dane puppy I've seen in over twenty-five years.

He was emaciated, the rachitic knobs on his ribs sticking out like a grotesque body necklace. Because of malnutrition, not only were his feet splayed and flattened to look like ducks' feet, but also his pasterns (ankles) were broken down. His dry coat came out in handfuls, his eyes were dull, and he was on the verge of giving up. I skipped the lecture on puppy mills and urged the couple to get him to a veterinarian right away, suggesting my own vet as one especially knowledgeable about Danes. But the folks getting their Dane from us weren't as forbearing as I was. They got their puppy while I was advising and plopped him down next to the waif.

"We come from Sacramento," they announced, "and this is the puppy we got right here in Fortuna. How much did you pay for yours?"

Turns out they paid $200 more for that poor, mistreated pup than our folks had for their ball of fire.

I did not get any follow-up on this story, except that they didn't go to my vet. Though I'm not a vet, my sense is that unless that puppy received intravenous feeding within twenty-four hours of when I saw him, he died.

Sad, sad, sad—and utterly avoidable—that story, yet there are thousands like it.

So don't go to a concentration camp to get a dog. Let's make these inhumane people go into a different business—one that doesn't deal in living creatures.

Chapter 4

Other Important Sources of Dogs

Anyone who cares deeply about dogs might adopt as a motto, "So many dogs—so little time." When you begin to add up all the sources from which you can get a dog, it seems as if they're everywhere. Even more important, we're learning that there's a dog for every reasonable need—dogs for the deaf, for the blind, for the elderly, and for people who are not fully mobile. Autistic children benefit from companionship with dogs, as do many people locked away in various kinds of mental illness.

In this chapter I'll deal with how to find the right dog from these other programs and sources:
1. Animal shelters
2. Rescue organizations
3. Dogs for the deaf
4. Dogs for mobility-impaired people
5. Dogs for the blind

As with any other program of acquiring a dog, in each case there are specific guidelines. Obviously, one must qualify to get a special-needs dog. Further, reputable shelters query prospective owners very closely before they begin the process of matching person with dog. In many states, puppies or dogs adopted from animal shelters must be spayed or neutered within a set period of time. The new owner pays a fee and signs a pledge to do this.

Animal Shelters

Until you visit or volunteer at your local animal shelter, you probably aren't aware of the enormous volume of puppies and dogs that a shelter deals with every day. I know that to me all this was abstract until I realized that I owed some payback to all the dogs that have mellowed my life, and I began to spend a day a week at the humane shelter. The biggest part of my work was as an adoption counselor, trying to get the right dog into the right home.

I was appalled.

Imagine a cage 4 feet by 8 feet (1.2 × 2.4 m), with a cement floor, chainlink walls, and a 2 foot by 4 foot

(.6 × 1.2 m) sleeping compartment at one end. Imagine two rows of these cages, stretching 100 feet (30.5 m), bisected by a narrow, cement-floored walkway. Now imagine how your favorite house dog would feel brought to one of these cages by a stranger and left, with strange dogs on either side and across the way, in a din of barking and howling and cage doors clanging shut. Twice a day, other strangers will bring in feed pans, clean the water dish, and clean out the cage, hosing all wastes down a central drain. Other strangers will come through, peering, talking, maybe coming into the cage and making advances to your dog, whom they will call by an alien name.

This describes our shelter, which was well run and commodious, as shelters go. Our kennel workers were humane folks, animal lovers all—and they burned out fast, which isn't surprising. In a good month we found homes for 50 percent of the dogs who came in. The rest were killed, or, as the paper trail indicated, PTS—Put To Sleep. I never decided whether it was less stressful to be out in the kennel area with the dogs or in the front office cleaning up reports. I never hardened to line after line where I had to fill in the notation "PTS." Nor was my heart warm toward the people who came through the front door lugging boxes of puppies or dragging old, sick dogs they didn't want any longer. In retrospect, I was more useful out in the kennels, for there I learned about the dogs we had who were ready for adoption.

Shelter workers do spend an increasing amount of time assessing dogs that can be released to new homes. Laws vary, but dogs picked up as strays by animal control officers must be held a certain length of time to allow their owners to find and redeem them. After that, depending on how crowded the shelter is, dogs who show an ability to adjust to a new home are kept so they may be adopted. Dogs turned into the shelter by their owners are eligible for adoption immediately if they seem able to make the adjustment.

Sick dogs don't make the cut. Old dogs often don't make the cut. Maimed dogs seldom live very long—it is, in the final analysis, kinder to kill a suffering dog than to keep it in pain hoping that some Florence Nightingale of dogs will magically appear and nurse it back to health. The only reason we got Stella, the maimed Dane who'd been in a leg trap for a couple of weeks, was because the kennelman on duty that day knew that we rescued Danes, and he wouldn't put her down until we had a chance to assess her. Often when a huge litter of puppies comes in, some are immediately put down because shelter personnel know they have no chance of being adopted. Unweaned puppies are put down unless some shelter worker takes them home and bottle-feeds them. Openly vicious dogs are put down.

Reputable shelters pair friendly, alert dogs with the right people.

So when you go to an animal shelter to find a puppy or a dog, you can start off knowing that a certain amount of culling has already taken place. You'll get to choose among the healthy dogs that have displayed enough socialization to convince shelter personnel that they can live successfully with people. It's smart to talk to one of the workers about exactly what you're looking for before you go to the kennel area to look at the dogs. For one thing, you'll probably want to spring every dog in the place once you see them, because most of them beg to be taken out. This is a situation when sympathy becomes almost overwhelming! Add your most generous impulses, and you're likely to come away with a dog you never dreamed of having. The shelter worker can guide you to dogs of the size, age, temperament, and general breed that you're looking for.

And yes, you can find purebred dogs and puppies at a shelter. It's likely that you'll have to wait, although if you're looking for one of the currently most popular breeds, your wait may be short. While I was working at the shelter, we apparently had some very active breeders of Dobermans, for there were always three or four available for adoption. These were not especially concerned breeders, as none came forth to rescue any dobies from us. One of the nightmares of the serious, longtime breeders of any breed is that some of their dogs that they thought they had sold to good homes end up unwanted at a shelter. That's why so many of them do breed rescue work.

Before you'll be allowed to take a dog from a shelter, you'll have to answer some questions and sign some pledges. Your previous pet history will be explored, and you'll be asked where you plan to keep your new pet. As I said, you'll have to get the dog spayed or neutered. You'll be asked about other pets you may already have. If you rent your home or apartment, you'll have to provide written proof that your landlord or landlady welcomes dogs. You'll be asked about fenced yards, pens, employment. Just as reputable breeders want to make sure the right dog goes to the right home, so do reputable shelters— perhaps with an even added desperation, because shelter dogs have already been failed once by people, and it's cruel to put them with more people who fail them.

Take your time at a shelter. Be guided by the folks who know something about each dog, but also be your own guide. Many shelters have fenced areas where you can visit with the dog(s) you're considering, away from the bedlam of the kennel area. Here you can assess your prospective pet's shyness or aggressiveness, responsiveness, interaction with you, trainability, and whatever subtle qualities cause one dog to say to you, "I'm yours!" It is absolutely true that you can teach many things to a shelter-obtained dog, but you are not going to be able to get the whole background on any dog you get from a shelter. Thus, what you see now is your starting point, and you need to assess carefully. Spend as much time as you need, for this is one situation when coming back tomorrow or the next day is likely not to work—the dog may be gone. If your shelter doesn't have a formal place where you can assess your potential dog, ask where you may go to be with your dog alone. Most shelter workers, be assured, want an adoption to work if you've qualified.

Most shelters wisely won't let you choose a dog for someone else, so if you're getting a dog for, say, an older relative, bring that person with you. It's the dog's potential owner who must qualify, not necessarily the person who takes the dog from the shelter. If you have children who'll be sharing your home with your dog, bring them. They'll be assessed, too. When I was volunteering, Brenda, one of our new workers, was faced with a woman and her mob of bratty children who were banging on cage doors, yelling to get dogs' attention, and being obviously unsocialized and uncontrollable.

"How am I going to tell that woman she doesn't qualify?" Brenda asked me.

"Pretend you're dealing with paperwork and eavesdrop," I told her. Introducing myself as the adoption counselor, I firmly told the woman that until her children were older, she was not a candidate to take a dog from the shelter.

She was outraged!

"Well!" she snapped. "I'll just come back another day."

I smiled my best shark's smile as she flounced out, yanking her brats with her, for I knew that we kept a blacklist, and my next act was going to be teaching Brenda how to use it.

You know and I know that if everyone that ever had a dog was qualified to have dogs, there wouldn't be the need for animal shelters.

What I never realized until I worked at the shelter is how amazingly trusting dogs are, and how forgiving. Time after time after time I saw dogs that had been abandoned go happily out of the shelter with their new owners, tails wagging and heads high, off to give people another chance to do the right thing.

Beware of. . .

A friend once got a dog through a private animal rescue service. She drove, in fact, several hundred miles to get the dog. His name was Prince (the infamous!), and he was, she was told, a miniature German Shepherd. (There's no such breed.) What he was was the dog from hell. He bit everyone in sight, including my friend. He was untrainable. Not only could he not be housebroken, he leaped around inside a car to the point of danger. My friend suffered with that dog for six months, never gaining an inch. He got her thrown out of every obedience class she enrolled them in. Her veterinarian made her muzzle Prince before he'd work on the dog. Life was a threat.

Finally, she did the responsible thing—she had Prince put down by her vet. That was a dog that never should have come up for adoption, and the people who run that private agency ought to have known as much. Because of bad breeding or bad socialization or abuse, there are incorrigible dogs. Whatever the reason, the responsible thing to do is to humanely kill them.

Unfortunately, there are well-meaning people who don't know—or won't accept—that fact. Some of them set out to rescue all dogs. My advice is that if you choose to give a home to a dog that needs one, go to a reputable humane society shelter. Your chances of getting just the right dog are excellent there.

Rescue Organizations

Having just blasted some privately run dog rescue organizations, now let me recommend specialized breed clubs who rescue only a given breed. Most major newspapers have ads placed by such groups. Many animal shelters have listings of breed rescuers.

People deeply committed to a given breed of dog devote their time, effort, and money to making sure that no worthy dog of their chosen breed has to be killed at an animal shelter. Breed rescues operate in many ways, from the kind of informal Dane rescue I've done for many years to well-built kennels maintained by some breed clubs to house abandoned dogs until they can be placed in the right new home. Both the rescued dogs and the prospective new owners are screened as carefully as they'd be if this were a good, ethical breeding kennel. Often prospective owners are screened more carefully than if they were getting a puppy, for rescue dogs, like shelter dogs, have already been traumatized by people and need new homes that can adapt to their special needs. I'd rather place a rescued Dane in a home that already knows Danes than in one new to the breed, because someone who has already lived with Danes knows what they're like and is prepared for some of their capers—like DJ's deciding to pitch into my friend for smacking her children!

What you get with a breed rescue club is contact with people who know a lot about whatever breed you're looking for. Often you'll be taken under the wing of a friendly breeder who can coach you through the early days when you don't know your dog very well. Each rescue organization makes its own rules. Many require that you spay or neuter your pet. Some charge; some don't. Most screen, so you won't get a vicious cocker spaniel or a corgi that kills small children and cats. I always assess any Dane that comes up for rescue, and I'm prepared to pay a veterinarian to humanely kill any Dane that's vicious or unfit to live with people, though I haven't met that Dane on the rescue circuit yet. The chances are that you won't get registration or a pedigree with a rescue dog; generally they aren't available, since when people abandon their dogs, they seldom tie the papers around the dog's neck. I have, however, gotten Danes turned into shelters complete with registrations and pedigrees! One of my current three dogs is a big brindle Dane bitch I rescued over four years ago. Sombra is a typical Dane; unhappy with the home she was in, she ran off and was picked up as a stray. When I got her, she was pregnant, though I didn't know it. After she had her puppies, I decided she didn't need to make another adjustment and integrated her into our home. Her name means "shadow" in Spanish, and she is, indeed, my shadow. The first week I had her, I was in the yard and momentarily didn't see her.

Keenly aware of how I had gotten her, I felt panic. "Where's Sombra?" I asked Kent in alarm.

"Look right behind you," he answered dryly.

Sure enough, pasted so close to me that I'd overlooked her in my quick scan, there was my shadow.

Beware of . . .

- Any person or organization that's too eager to push off on you any dog they know little about.
- Any person or organization that claims there are never dogs that aren't fit for human companionship.
- Any place where you can get a dog with absolutely no questions asked of you—these people aren't working in the best interests of dogs or of the people who live with them.

Dogs for the Deaf

Sometimes called hearing dogs, these special needs dogs provide an amazing service to people. There are many organizations now that train dogs to be the ears for people who can't hear and thus keep them living fairly normal lives in a home setting. I've listed two of the training

When the dog is old enough, it begins an intensive four- to six-month training period at a center run by the organization. Each organization has its own set of very specific verbal and/or hand commands that the dogs learn. Hearing dogs in general learn to respond to several sounds: knocking at a door; a doorbell or buzzer; an alarm clock; smoke alarms; telephones; a baby crying; an oven buzzer, and a name being called. They lead their deaf partners to the source of the sound they're responding to. As the dogs progress, their trainers further evaluate them, for there are several levels of proficiency for hearing dogs:

1. The Certified Hearing Dogs are trained to work with their partners in public as well as at home. They have legal access to stores, public transportation, restaurants, schools, and workplaces, just as guide dogs for the blind do.

2. Working Companion Dogs are also obedience trained and taught to respond to sounds, but they work only in their partners' homes or other private places; they do not have public access rights.

3. Social Dogs have shown themselves to be not suited for the kinds of advanced training the previous two categories of dogs can handle. They are obedience trained and often placed with deaf children to teach them how to care for a dog and to ready them for a more advanced dog later. Social Dogs may also be

groups in the Other Resources Appendix at the back of this book (see page 91).

One of the most exciting aspects of some hearing dog programs is that the trainers find their dogs at animal shelters. Often the dogs are mixed breeds, small to medium in size. Each is evaluated by trainers from the program. Qualities like friendliness, curiosity, intelligence, and an energetic nature are important. Good health is, of course, a necessity. Puppies as well as mature dogs may be chosen for the program. Young pups—under eight months of age—go to the homes of volunteer puppy raisers where they are socialized and given whatever obedience training that particular program requires.

placed with people who need well-trained companions to better their quality of life, for instance with older people, or with children who have developmental disabilities.

The final phase of each dog's training must be done in the home of the recipient, for the dog has to know how to respond to the specific sounds of that home. Follow-up is provided by the organization, and the progress of the human/canine team is monitored. Occasionally an inappropriate match is made, which is corrected either by teaming with a different dog, or, in rare cases, by deciding that the service dog situation isn't working.

As is the case with all organizations that train and place special needs dogs, the need is greater than the supply of trained dogs. Most organizations depend for their operation on contributions, grants, fund raisers, and volunteer contributions of work, money, and time. Many do not charge the recipients of these marvelous dogs more than a small fraction of what it costs to get the dogs trained. Most organizations have long waiting lists of qualified recipients.

Nor does every deaf or hearing-impaired person qualify as a partner for a dog. First, of course, the person must love and respect dogs. He or she must recognize the need for the services a trained dog can provide and be willing to provide the kinds of in-home training that will keep the dog's responses sharp. There must be no other dogs in the household. The dog's human partner must be willing to provide a fenced yard or pen for the dog, plus adequate exercise, proper grooming, good diet, and necessary veterinary care. The dog will have been spayed or neutered before it's placed with its human partner. If the person is under 18 the rest of the family must qualify to make the program work.

But for the person who qualifies and gets a Certified Hearing Dog, consider the freedom such a partnership provides! No longer alone in a silent world, vulnerable and restricted, a deaf person is now free to shop, go to restaurants or ball games, ride the bus or fly across the world, and be partnered in a life of rewarding work. And for the dog, once an abandoned stray in a shelter, perhaps awaiting euthanasia, now it is a vital teammate in someone's life.

Meko in close-up.

Dogs for the Mobility-impaired

I've visited Canine Companions for Independence (CCI), which was started in Santa Rosa, California, in 1975 by Dr. Bonita Bergin, an American schoolteacher. From her small beginning of one dog and one quadriplegic woman has grown one of the most sophisticated dog training organizations in the world. In 1992, CCI graduated 103 teams of human/canine partners. CCI dogs lead to independent living people with an amazing range of impairments by being their hands, their feet, and their ticket to full participation in life. Back in 1975, it was estimated that the Service Dog Dr. Bergin trained saved his partner $30,000 every year in companion-

The therapeutic value of dogs is a subject just barely understood.

care costs. There's no way anyone can calculate what these dogs give to their teammates in the way of self-confidence, freedom, and integration into mainstream living. Yet CCI depends entirely on donations, grants, fund raisers, and the work of volunteers to raise its money.

The first thing that hit me when I approached the Santa Rosa training center was the happy sight of several golden retrievers playing together in a large fenced area. It was, I was told, recess time. Released from their morning's work and under the eye of one of the trainers, these young golden dogs chased balls, romped with each other, and announced my arrival with big yaps. They were obviously bursting with health and high spirits, well-socialized dogs that had no need to savage each other, run from strangers, or sulk in corners.

CCI now depends almost entirely on their own breeding stock. Besides the golden retrievers, they use Labrador retrievers and Pembroke Welsh Corgis. With their controlled breeding program, CCI is able to predict not only the basic soundness of their dogs, but also the temperament. Breeding stock lives with "breeder caretakers" throughout their lives, under careful veterinarian guidelines and supervision. Puppies come to the national veterinary center when they're seven weeks old. There they are examined, temperament-tested, and permanently marked for identification.

From there, the puppies go to one of the five regional training centers, where they are temporarily adopted by volunteer puppy raisers. They will stay with their puppy raiser until they're 18 months old.

The major task of puppy raisers is to socialize these pups. I was just delighted to discover that one of the rules a puppy raiser must agree to is that the puppy shall sleep in your bedroom with you right from the start, as I've always believed that this is where a puppy belongs if the optimum bond with humans is to be formed. CCI says that the puppies are learning their future jobs even while they are sleeping, for their job will require them to be present for their human teammate day and night. But besides the socializing aspect of raising a CCI puppy, there's more. CCI dogs have to be alert, confident, able to work in distracting circumstances, and used to the world at large, so a puppy raiser has to make sure the pup gets out and about. Right from the start, CCI puppies wear special capes with the CCI logo. These serve two purposes:

1. To accustom the puppy to something on its back during "work" hours so it can easily acclimate later on to the back-pack it will wear.
2. To identify the puppy so it gains access to public places where dogs usually are not allowed. Added to this unusual out-and-about regime are regular obedi-

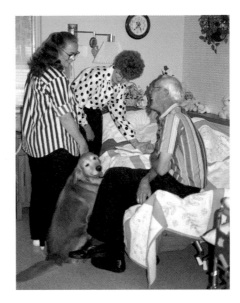

Specially trained dogs extend people's independence, as well as providing companion-ship.

ence classes, approved by CCI, so by the time the puppy is 18 months old and ready for the next step in its training, it knows about 50 commands.

When the pup returns to the regional training center at 18 months, again it's temperament-tested and evaluated by a veterinarian. The pups that qualify enter another six-month course of advanced training. The dogs I saw were in that advanced stage. Because of CCI's careful breeding program, the percentage of dogs that qualify for advanced training is very high. The few who do not qualify, however, are returned to their puppy raiser families or adopted out to community members. During the advanced training, dogs work with trainers who, acting as the disabled with whom the dogs will eventually be paired, use wheelchairs, crutches, ramps, no hand signals, and none of the kinds of body language many of us take for granted. By the end of this time, each dog will know at least 100 commands. Dogs are carefully monitored. The best of the best go back into the breeding program. The others go into one of four categories:

1. Service Dogs assist individuals who are physically disabled. Typically, they push elevator buttons, turn lights on and off, retrieve dropped items, get things out of cupboards and refrigerators, open doors, and pull wheelchairs. They help people who have been disabled from spinal cord injury, multiple sclerosis, polio, cerebral palsy, muscular dystrophy, arthritis, or stroke. Service Dogs have full legal access to all public places, as do Guide Dogs for the Blind.

2. Signal Dogs, or hearing dogs. Corgis are used for this work at CCI. Since they don't have to reach for the kinds of tasks the labs and goldens do, their size makes them excellent for this kind of work. Their innate herding instinct is used to help them get their human partner to the source of the sound.

3. Social Dogs work with individuals who are developmentally disabled, autistic, or convalescing. I learned that the line between a Service Dog and a Social Dog is very fine. The one factor that's different is that a Social Dog doesn't have as many public access rights as a Service Dog. A Social Dog may also work in institutions such as nursing homes.

4. Specialty Dogs are custom-trained for people who have multiple disabilities—for instance, someone who is both deaf and disabled, as a person who has had a stroke might be.

After their advanced training, CCI dogs are ready for that last step—being paired with the person who will be their partner. In a two-week period called Team Training (but referred to by participants as Boot Camp!), qualified recipients come to regional centers to learn how to interact with their Service Dogs or their Social Dogs. Staff persons study dogs and people to make good matches. Stubborn dogs are paired with stubborn people, and the aggressive dogs go to aggressive people. This isn't accomplished immediately. Participants work with different dogs as staff watch carefully for the right match. At every turn of the way, CCI training builds on the dog's basic strengths instead of trying to turn the dog into something it isn't. Now, in days lasting from eight to ten hours and under the tutelage of CCI trainers, people and dogs become teams. This is an intensive time for the participants, for they have to learn tons of information about the care, handling, and training of their Canine Companion. On top of that, they have to learn to risk, for the basic point of this entire program is independence. Thus, each participant must pass a shopping mall test alone with his or her Canine Companion, for example, before graduation.

Signal Dogs and Specialty Dogs get their last-step training in the homes where they'll be working. Particularly for Specialty Dogs, the recipient may be too severely disabled to undergo the rigors of Team Training. The Signal Dog, as with any hearing dog, needs to learn to respond to the idiosyncratic sounds of the home it'll be working in.

Canine Companions for Independence has a three to four year waiting list, so great is the need for these dogs. Although the person getting the dog pays only $125, the cost of a CCI dog "from insemination to graduation," as Nina, who briefed me, put it, is $10,000. And because the program graduates dogs who literally have their human's life in their paws, the process of training is a long and careful one. But when you think of a child who can lead a fairly normal life in spite of spina bifida with the help of his or her Canine Companion, or the adult who can live and work independently because of a wonderful dog trained by people with a mission, you realize that there's a whole world of dogs out there that far transcends just getting a puppy on a whim from a cute little kid who has a box of fluffballs outside a supermarket.

I've included how to reach Canine Companions for Independence in the Resources section. Besides the possibility that someone reading this book may qualify for a Canine Companion, there's also the possibility that you just adore puppies and would like nothing better than to be one of CCI's puppy raisers. Indeed, without the puppy raisers, the program could not be as big as it is.

Two major impressions stay with me having visited CCI. One is the joyous dogs, working confidently with their trainers. The other is a deep knowledge that every dog is happier when it has a job to do, knows what that job is, and is trained to do the job. The reason, it seems to me, that dogs have been such a vital part of human history is that they have constantly made our lives better, happier, easier, and more meaningful. We may not be as aware of how much we depend on our casual canine companions as the recipients of a CCI dog are, but for each of us, in its own way, our dog does a job for us.

And we owe all the same commitments to our dogs that the folks at CCI demand of those who would partner with one of their superstars.

Dogs for the Blind

Of all the special needs dogs, Guide Dogs for the Blind are the best known. In California, Guide Dogs for the Blind, Inc. was established in

German shepherds are the most commonly recognized Guide Dogs.

1942. Currently the organization, a nonprofit school, is located in San Rafael, California, operating under License #1 from the California State Guide Dog Board.

The mission of this school is "To aid and assist blind persons through the use of trained dogs." Any legally blind person over age sixteen who is physically and temperamentally suited to use a guide dog may apply for in-residence training, which takes 28 days.

Like Canine Companions, Guide Dogs for the Blind (GDB) depends on its own breeding program. Three breeds are used: golden retrievers, Labrador retrievers, and German shepherds. These three breeds are each big enough to guide a person; have medium coats, so are adaptable to all kinds of climates; and have consistently shown an eagerness to work and a steady temperament. GDB depends heavily on 4-H members as puppy raisers, placing puppies in their puppy rais-

ing families at three months. After 12 to 18 months, the dog returns to the San Rafael facility where it joins a "string" of 28 to 30 dogs. Each string is under the supervision of a state-licensed instructor. The dogs spend at least four months in this advanced training, which includes basic obedience work and progresses into guiding people in traffic, on busy streets, in elevators, and on public transportation. Guide Dogs have full legal access to public facilities and are well enough known that their human teammates are seldom challenged any longer. About 50 percent of the dogs from this program graduate to Guide Dog status. Of the rest, some go into the breeding program, and the others are either adopted back into their puppy-raising family or go to someone else.

One interesting facet of Guide Dog training is that the dogs are taught when to disobey commands. If safety would be compromised by obeying the command, the dog must refuse. You can see that the person getting such a dog would have to learn how to "read" the dog closely to distinguish between plain sloppiness and proper behavior. GDB staff emphasizes that the dogs have to want to do the work they do. Like Canine Companions, Guide Dogs work for praise and love. Both kinds of dogs are taught with positive reinforcement rather than harsh corrections, yet corrections must be done.

GDB runs 12 classes a year training recipients with dogs. The 28-day school is intensive, working from initial drill to off-site experiences in San Rafael and, finally, to the busiest parts of San Francisco. I can only imagine what kind of trust and risk-acceptance these excursions demand! Dogs sleep in the school's dormitory with their people and accompany them to meals, preparing for the kind of closeness a Guide Dog and its person will have. Like CCI, GDB studies each class to match the right dog with the right person. Again we see the importance of working with the dog's basic nature. Surely these two professional groups that deal with people whose very independence hinges on their dogs show the rest of us why it is folly, indeed, to acquire a pup by accident or on whim.

Guide Dogs for the Blind, Inc., depends for funding on the same kinds of donations, fund raisers, grants, and volunteer activities the other special-needs dog organizations look to. GDB also does not charge recipients for their dogs. I've included information on how to contact GDB in the Resources section (page 91). Here's another spot where, if you love raising puppies and can bear to give them up, you could provide a needed service.

* * *

The more we learn about ourselves as people and about animals as thinking, planning individuals, the more we're going to see new ways to pair us and our dogs. As the old master-slave relationship between person and dog disappears, and we think more in terms of complementing each other's shortcomings, we're going to find more good jobs for our canine partners. Someday, we hope, we'll close down the shelters because there won't be any more abandoned pets; humans will have chosen their dogs and cats so carefully that they'd never think of parting with them.

Chapter 5

Which Dog Do I Take?

As we saw in the last chapter, the people who match special needs people with trained dogs are very picky about making sure the match is a good one. The nature of the dog and the nature of the person are considered, so that an energetic dog isn't paired with a reticent person, or a dominant dog with a passive person. Though a dog's basic nature can be modified, it's smart to begin with a dog whose nature you want to enhance. Living with a dog is a lot like a marriage; smart people pick as spouses people they like, not people they think they can change into people they like! The reason there are so many breeds of dogs is that there are so many kinds of people. Even within the breeds there is, as I've pointed out, an allowable spectrum of temperament.

With the exception of the special needs dog, any dog or puppy you choose should visit your veterinarian within 24 hours. If your pup is well, your vet sees it when it's well and talks over future immunizations and the subject of spaying or neu-

tering with you. If the dog is defective, as was the case with a family that got a deaf dalmatian recently, you need to take it back before you get further attached. If it's running a little temperature, perhaps due to stress, you need to nip that in the bud. My experience has always been splendid with my dogs' veterinarians, and I believe you can do yourself and your new pet no greater favor than establishing your partnership with your vet as soon as possible.

Puppy Signs

When you get an eight-week-old puppy, you forego knowing as much about your dog when grown as you would if you aquire the puppy at a more advanced age. Yet you also will have the greatest influence over what your adult will be like, because you'll do all the initial bonding and training. That's a challenge and a threat, because if the adult turns out to be a pill, you did it!

Physically all puppies should exhibit common signs of good health. Clear eyes tell you a lot about diet and cleanliness of the pup's environment. Puppies should be well-fleshed, but not fat. At eight weeks, their ribs should be well covered, with only a hint at where the bones are. Puppy coats are usually fuzzy. Often it isn't until late adolescence that the gleam of good health shines through the coat when all the puppy fuzz sheds away. However, patchy or matted coats tell of lack of grooming and cleanliness, as well as of poor nutrition. While puppies are still nursing, their mothers clean them wth their tongues. Some mothers are more conscientious than others. We've had both kinds: Starshine, who just about scrubbed the hide off her pups, and Barbarella, who considered that once she had fed the little wretches, she had done almost more than could be expected. Obviously, we had to work harder to keep Barbarella's puppies presentable than we did with Starshine's.

However, we got to know Barbarella's puppies faster than we did Star's, and they were socialized to people faster because of all the handling they required. Thus they responded to prospective buyers more enthusiastically and were an easier "sell." No matter what you have in mind for your adult dog, you want a puppy that responds positively to people. The intensity of this positive response varies from

breed to breed. Terrier pups are more likely to come boiling over to greet you than, say, saluki pups, because salukis are a restrained dog by nature. Although Dane pups will come to look you over, some of them won't stay long, because basically Danes like their immediate family much better than they do anyone else. This is true of the working and herding dogs in general; however, once you become their person, you get their full attention. Knowledgeable breeders won't force a puppy to go to new people. There is a chemistry that happens, and it's wise to observe that chemistry. Ruffiana, a pushy harlequin Dane puppy, refused to have anything to do with people who came looking at her and her sibs. She had made up her mind from the start that she belonged to Kent and me—and, yes, we kept her.

As you observe puppies in a litter, you can see dominant pups and submissive ones. This does not follow gender lines. Sometimes size will show you dominance, as the bigger ones are the ones who have

A batch of healthy, exuberant German shepherd puppies.

Puppies go through some amusing stages, as this German shepherd pup with a skewed ear demonstrates.

unbearable racket when they think it's feeding time. When asleep, they twitch and jerk and yip. What you will not hear in a litter of healthy puppies is prolonged whining. You also do not want to hear coughing, as that means illness. Nor do you want to hear fruity, mucus-laden snuffling, though you'll hear fruitier breathing from brachycephalic pups like boxers or English bull-dogs than you will from the long-nosed breeds.

Breeders speak of "puppy breath." It's an idiosyncratic smell, sharp and acrid, with an undertang of urine, that all healthy puppies have. You either like it or you don't, and it doesn't matter, because all puppies also outgrow puppy breath. Often it's necessary to clean pups up, but because of the chill factor associated with a full-scale bath, many breeders use one of the commercial "quick clean" products that can be toweled on messy spots and easily dried off. So you might smell a piney scent. Keeping puppies clean in a litter situation is a challenge. They immediately climb into their food pans when dinner is presented. They will walk through one pan to get to the vastly better food in the identical pan down the way. Or they get bowled over into the pan by the bully of the family. Even in the litter-box, puppies won't eliminate where they eat or sleep, but they're obscenely curious and will toddle over to see what another puppy has

been muscling their way to the best food supply. You can also tell about dominance by who hogs the toys. But at eight weeks, puppies have socialized mainly with each other and their mother. Their power plays have been among canines. Now they are just beginning to turn their attention to people, sizing us up. The hell-raiser of the litter does not necessarily become the fireball as an adult. Barbarella was a good example of this. She beat up all the other pups in her litter, got the best of everything, and always came out on top. But as an adult, she was a wimp. She was easy to train, got along well with other dogs, and saw no reason to push. I was hugely disappointed in her!

Besides looking at pups, listen to them, smell them, and feel them with your hands. Healthy puppies make a lot of noise when they're awake. They yap, puppy-growl at each other, have mock fights that they take very seriously as long as they can remember what they're doing. They yelp, and set up an eliminated, getting themselves dirtied in the process. Now that Kent and I aren't breeding Danes any longer, we have this backlog of semi-decent bath towels. We never used to have any, because a litter of puppies always cleaned us out of all but our most recently purchased towels. I'd take an armful of towels with me whenever I went to feed puppies—damp towels for getting off stubborn food, dry towels for keeping off the chills, towels moistened with Skip-Bath for stinky spots. I washed a lot of gunky towels in those days.

Any sign of sores, especialy on a puppy's belly, tells you the pup hasn't been kept clean. Puppies' skins are very sensitive to dirt and tattle of poor hygiene.

Although all puppies do not appreciate being picked up, once you've begun to settle on *your* puppy, ask to hold it. Put one hand securely under its bottom and back legs and hold it gently but close. You should feel a lot of squirming, a generous double handful of active, lively, healthy puppy. This is entirely unscientific, but a well puppy or dog simply feels good to the hand. The skin is supple and elastic, there are no sharp bones protruding, and there's abundant life that you can feel. How much a pup struggles or relaxes when being held is, again, a matter of breed and temperament. But puppies shouldn't become hysterical at being held. That shows a pup that's going to be difficult to socialize. Be

sure you want that kind of difficulty before choosing such a pup.

While you have the pup in hand, check the ears. They should be clean and supple. Check the mouth. The gums should be a healthy pink (except in certain breeds, like the chow). The puppy will perhaps struggle some at being thus checked over, but the amount and quality of the struggling tells you some more about how cooperative this kid is going to be when you come to establishing your dominance. You are, at this point, deciding whether the two of you are going to be able to live successfully and harmoniously together.

You should be able to do this kind of watch, listen, smell, and feel with puppies you're considering, whether you're dealing with a serious breeder, a backyard breeder, or the local humane shelter. There have been numerous "tests" put

Great Dane puppies in their food pan.

A mother pug with her puppy.

out purporting to teach you how to judge by "scientific" measures what a puppy will become. I find them mainly faddish and pop. You've done enough thinking, studying, and observing by now that your own common sense, plus a few health and temperament guidelines, will enable you to choose your own puppy very handily.

Beware of . . .

- The puppy that runs and hides. This shows excessive shyness, and excessively shy puppies often grow up to be fear-biters. Prince was probably such a puppy.
- The purebred puppy that is significantly smaller than the rest. Not all litters have a "runt." Small size may indicate only that the pup hasn't been getting its share of the food. It probably indicates a passive nature, which is what some people want. Check it out to make sure it doesn't mean the puppy's sick. This size differential isn't as significant in a mixed-breed litter, as dogs from such

parentage generally aren't uniform.
- The sickly puppy. Sick puppies can be made well, but a small, shy, sickly puppy may be sickly all its life. Be sure you are ready to live with such a canine before you let sympathy rule you.

Sight Unseen?

The national dog magazines are full of ads for purebred dogs. You may see just what you think you want, but the pup may be 2,000 miles away. Can you take the chance that the puppy will be the right one?

I give a qualified "yes."

With the advent of camcorders, many breeders are videotaping their litters and sending the tapes, often at a price to be refunded if you buy a puppy. So you can sort of see the pups. I say "sort of" because getting puppies to do anything useful for pictures is a losing proposition. Kent and I came closer to divorce during puppy picture-taking sessions than at any other time in our lives. I have a box full of virtually identical pictures of oddly posed, gawky little blue, black, or harlequin Dane puppies, all originally supposed to be "show stacked" poses for prospective owners! I have candids of litter boxes occupied by busy little bugs doing whatever they were feeling like doing at the time.

There was a time when we flew puppies all over the country to new homes, and it was a very stressful time. First, we qualified the prospective new owners by mail and phone. Then there were the exchanges of pictures, and they qualified us and the pup. Finally, there was the day-before-flying physical at our veterinarian's, the phone calls to corroborate the puppy's flight plan, and the trip to the airport. Neither Kent nor I ever left before we actually saw the plane take off, for we had one more phone call to make, the one that said, "Your puppy is actually in the air, and the flight bill number is . . ." Neither of us ever left the airport dry-eyed, either, I might add. Then there was a fast drive home to sit by the phone and await the phone call that announced, "My puppy is here; she made the trip well, and she's just what I wanted." When we shipped adult dogs too big to go out of our regional airport, the dog would arrive at its new home, wherever that might be in the country, before I got back from the five-and-a-half-hour drive from San Francisco. I'd burst into the house exhausted and ask Kent, "Everything OK?"

I learned to fly dogs from some pros who flew show dogs all over the country. But flying is always stressful on a dog or puppy, so I always worried, though we never lost a one. I dealt with really concerned, humane, helpful people at the various airline baggage terminals way off on the backsides of airports, people who did everything in their power to minimize the trauma of the event for the dogs, and I appreciate their going the extra steps that made dogs more secure.

I also always worried about whether I had *really* picked the right puppy, whether what I called "excellent" would meet the new owners' expectations, or whether the poor pup would have to turn right around and fly back. That never happened, either.

You want to make sure that whatever the pictures show (and even with camcorders, puppies all look pretty much alike at a certain age), you learn from your source what your puppy's temperament is like. Information must flow freely in both directions. When I'd get a query like, "I want a pet-quality,

Adult Kuvasz with puppies.

solid black male Dane, guaranteed to be no less than 36 inches (92 cm) at the shoulder at adulthood, hips guaranteed, and with perfect, dark eyes; I do not plan to show or breed him," I knew I was being conned. I seldom had such a pup at that moment! And you want to know that if you're being offered a guarantee of world-class quality at some world-class price, you're getting the straight scoop, not a scam. If you don't feel comfortable with the people from whom you're proposing to get a long-distance dog, wait for another dog. There are scam artists.

For every long-distance transaction, the seller should be more concerned about the dog's well-being and flight time than yours. As I used to say to people, "You can get out of the car, go have a bite to eat, stretch your legs. Your puppy is in a flight crate, all alone, and scared. I've routed him on as quick a flight as there is, even though you'll have to drive an hour to get him." Ask every question you can think of about how much experience the puppy-seller has with flying dogs. Make sure every possible fail-safe is built into the flight plan. Get to the airport early.

Prepare to unravel. Kent had to restrain me when Starshine flew in from Chicago. The baggage crew left her in her flight crate out on the runway while they loaded an outgoing flight. I could see her jumping around, so I knew her tranquilizer had worn off. Even where we were, the noise was headpounding. And there was my eight-week-old new puppy being ignored amid all the din! I was going to go get her, since the incompetents who were supposed to get her out of that racket weren't doing so. Fortunately, Star came joyously out of her crate, washing us both with her tongue and teething enthusiastically on any hand she could reach. She played the entire 45-minute drive home, casually cleaned the cats out of food as she crossed the back porch on the way into the house, demanded a snack, and eventually had to be put back into her crate so the people could get some sleep that night.

Yes, you can get a very fine dog or puppy from across the country if you're dealing with the right people. I've been on both ends of that bargain.

The Older Dog

You know that I believe there's a lot to be said for getting a dog that's already started. My learning about how the folks at Canine Companions for Independence and Guide Dogs for the Blind don't even put their dogs into the final stages of training until they're about two years old only corroborated what I already know: there's no reason to hesitate about getting an adult dog. Remember, too, that these special dogs from CCI and GDB make their most important bond *after* several changes in family and living situation.

If you get an adult dog from an ethical breeder, you'll know everything you need to know—and maybe more!—about your dog's idiosyncrasies. If you get your dog from a shelter, you'll know no more than the shelter personnel do, but at least you'll know present temperament, size, and looks. In my experience, the most difficult dog to cope with is the adolescent. Like children of junior high school age, they're just beginnng to feel their hormones, and they're pushing the limits as far as who is boss. The untrained adolescent big dog is a handful that tests the skills of even the most experienced dog owner.

While your every task with the puppy is to establish good habits, with an older dog, you'll probably have to break some bad ones. DJ's daughter, Emily, was a joy and a delight but she grew up to be entirely too refined for either showing or breeding. When Flora, a single mother with several children, came seeking a Dane, I introduced her to Emily, then around three years old. Emily adored children, puppies, kittens. She and Flora took to each other immediately. Flora brought the children to visit,

The new dog needs to be integrated into the family.

and Emily and they were a match. Emily went to visit at Flora's home and was happy. So the day came when Emily moved permanently to Flora's. I knew she faced a happier life as an only dog, not one of many. Flora later told me that the biggest adjustment for her as a mother was to discover that she'd acquired not just a dog, but also a babysitter with very strict rules! No fighting among the children was the most inflexible rule. Emily broke up the squabbles by planting herself between the offending children, sometimes having to tug at a piece of clothing to interrupt the argument. To some, this behavior of Emily's might have been something to change. Flora found it highly acceptable, as she did Emily's habit of rounding up the children when she thought it was their bedtime.

Chapter 6
Home at Last

You've made your choice and have brought your new puppy or dog home. Now, it's up to you, as the leader of the pack (which you call your family) to help this charming bundle of impulses become a civilized member of your family.

Here, I'm going to pay particular attention to some common problems you might run into with an older dog. For youngsters, of course I strongly recommend that you purchase a copy of *Civilizing Your Puppy*.

Housebreaking

The single bad habit that gets more dogs banished than any other is a refusal to become housebroken. If this is what you inherited with an adult dog, you must begin all over, just as if you were dealing with a puppy before housebreaking even began. You have an edge, because an adult dog can learn more quickly than a puppy. Furthermore, the adult has greater bowel and bladder control. Plan to invest three active days in housebreaking. Be firm, and praise your dog for doing what any sensible dog would be doing. Be

prompt and equally firm in scolding any infraction.

There are three main reasons for adult dogs' not being housebroken:
1. Nobody ever taught them.
2. Hostility.
3. Insecurity.

Let's see how to spot each.
1. Nobody taught the dog to be houseclean. If this was the case, training is easy. If your otherwise cooperative dog messes in the house and appears surprised that you object, you're undoubtedly looking at a case of missing training. Get a solid book on puppy training and follow the instructions. I recommend *Civilizing Your Puppy* (and why shouldn't I, since I wrote it). With an adult, skip the paper training step.
2. Hostility. If your dog looks you in the eye and deliberately hikes his leg on the sofa, you're being dared. Ths is more difficult to cope with, but the issue here isn't housetraining—it's dominance. You have every right and reason to be furious and to show it. Smack the dog with a newspaper or zap it with a water pistol and take it—on leash—outside.

Stay until the dog eliminates, praise profusely, and go back inside. As your dog bonds more and more with you, and as you establish that you are and always will be top dog, boss, *alpha* in this outfit, such behavior will disappear.

3. Insecurity. Of the three, I find this one the hardest to cope with. In this group you find the submissive dog that piddles on the floor at the first sign that someone looks at her cross-eyed. The issue is still dominance, but in this case, your dog doesn't have enough of it! You need to build up her self-confidence, but in the meantime, you also need to provide an environment in which her accidents are unlikely to happen. Here's where a crate is a godsend, as dogs do not mess where they sleep. Further, watch for special occasions when she is insecure enough to piddle and whisk her cheerfully outdoors to eliminate. The cheer and upbeat praise are factors in building her self-confidence. With increased confidence, the unacceptable behavior will disappear.

Running Away

A second bad habit that gets dogs impounded is running away. A dog wanders for several reasons. Three of the most common are:

1. It hasn't been taught to stay home.

2. It is escaping a bad or abusive home.

3. It's an incorrigible wanderer. Let's see what can be done.

1. The dog that simply hasn't been taught is the easiest one to cure of wanderlust. You do not provide an opportunity for the dog to leave your property except on leash and with you or some other family member. Plan to observe your new dog carefully for a few days. If you see that it appears not to respond to a "Come!" command, you probably have an untaught canine. Keep the dog on leash or in a fenced yard until it responds promptly and dependably to "Come!," then widen the horizons of where you train your dog to come. Dogs of the sporting and hound groups need more thorough training in coming when called and staying in their yards than dogs of the working or herding groups. Any new dog that you get needs to be taught what its boundaries are. This process can take as little as a weekend or as much as several months, depending on breed, stubbornness, and your insistence. In retrospect, I'd say that Joli, my happy wanderer, was a dog that wasn't properly taught from puppyhood on to stay on his own turf. So he made his rounds when my back was turned, but always came home for supper.

2. Many dogs get bad homes, and some of them leave those homes as soon as they can. When I was at the shelter and saw a working or a herding dog brought in for straying, I generally suspected something amiss in the dog's home. Every Dane that I've rescued has come from a bad situation, and every one has responded to a loving home by sticking to it like a burr to a spaniel's ear. There's still that time of teaching boundaries, but the dog you rescue from a bad home is going to want to stay with you. Do basic training for coming when called, of course.

3. The incorrigible wanderer is another story. I've known more dogs than bitches to have this problem, and for dogs the cure is direct and simple—neutering. Dogs respond to the enticing scent of a bitch in heat even though she may be miles away. Once they've been neutered and their hormones are no longer driving them, they're more likely to stay home. However, such dogs always need supervision, for their wandering habits become deeply ingrained. We kenneled my friend Monique's lab cross, Brahms, when she went on vacation. Brahms had been a wanderer, but he had been neutered and his footloose days were, we all believed, behind him. Ha! Kent went in to clean Brahms' pen, Brahms slipped past him like a

fleeing shadow, and the dog was gone. Wonderful! How do I tell my friend that I've managed to lose her dear dog that she left with me for safekeeping? Fortunately Kent and I know how to think like a dog, and we guessed that Brahms had gone looking for Monique. Sure enough—clear across town, there was Brahms, sniffing around the company grounds where Monique worked. Having not located Monique, he was glad to see us, his friends, but it was a tense time until Monique returned from vacation and claimed her brilliant escape artist.

Though I said that dogs are more prone to wandering than bitches, a bitch in heat will slip away looking for an unsuitable mate. At the peak of her heat period, a bitch can get very clever in finding ways to escape, so if you get a purebred bitch that is so valuable as breeding stock that you don't want her spayed, either provide a safe environment for her during her heats, or kennel her where there is such a safe place.

There are canine escape artists that defy categorizing. Often they are highly intelligent, curious, easily bored dogs who go looking for excitement. Our Dane Chief was such a dog. It was bad enough that he'd take a slip whenever he could, but even worse, his favorite playmate, Minerva, was always up for going along on one of Chief's adventures. A pair of running Danes can not only cover a lot of ground in a short time; they also frighten people. Kent learned to build very tight pens because of Chief and Minerva. I do truly believe that if you get the escape artist who absolutely has to see what's on the other side of the hill, your only recourse is to thwart that desire with a tightly fenced yard or a good pen. Chief was a great dog to take on an outing to the beach or the river under our supervision, because he was fulfilling his love of travel and adventure, yet he didn't stray from our view. We never took Chief *and* Minerva together to the beach, for they were too tuned to each other and likely to go roaming. Minerva got to go on trips with more placid dogs who didn't respond to her itchy feet.

Leash Training

Another common reason adult dogs or older puppies end up at shelters is that no one took the time to leash train them. There comes a time when leash training is a difficult task, and often people find themselves not committed enough to their dog to go through the hassle. At the shelter, we generally didn't consider lack of leash training sufficient reason to kill an otherwise nice-tempered dog. If we had enough volunteers, we did some leash training before the dog was offered for adoption. Otherwise, we chose potential new owners carefully, and let them know what they were in for.

Leash training is important. Best done at an early age, it can be successfully taught to an older dog.

If you adopt a shelter dog that isn't leash trained, get thee to an obedience class as soon as possible. In a controlled environment and with the help of a trainer who has dealt with lots of problem dogs, you'll have the support and added knowledge you need to remedy the problem. Leash training is another of those dominance matters between humans and canines. Dogs at either end of the

Once the dog has learned the Heel, you can progress to the Sit...

dominant/submissive spectrum are equally difficult to leash train. The excessively dominant ones fight it because they recognize that a leash means control. The overly submissive ones dissolve into puddles of quivering despair and have to be jollied into enough confidence to be able to get up on all four feet and walk proudly beside you on leash.

and the Stay.

Dominance

There are people who get more dog than they bargained for, not only because the dog is bigger than they expected, but also because the dog is more dominant than they're able or willing to cope with. Such dogs can fit well into the right situation, but the issue of dominance is very important. If you're a strong, dominant person, you probably won't like and might even intimidate a wimpy dog. Chances are you can cope with a lot of dog, no matter the size. Certain breeds take more active corrective training than others. Terriers, for instance, are generally self-motivated and need to be forcefully taught what *you* consider acceptable behavior. Most working and herding dogs are closely tuned to their owners and pick up your cues about behavior with little need for lots of reinforcement. And to everything there are exceptions.

My most recent Dane, Cordy, whom I got when he was seven months old, is the most dominant Dane I've ever known. His breeder told me that Cordy "makes up his own mind whether or not to obey." After living with him for a few days, I realized that Cordy viewed himself as the boss dog and was not eager to cede that status to a mere human. I saw the most definite sign of his dominance one day when he got up on the couch next to me, sat his rear end on the back of the couch so he towered over me, and proceeded to smack me with his front paw. I do not like to rough-house with enormous puppies. Verbal commands produced no results, so I stood up quickly, with determination in my body language. Cordy stopped pawing at me immediately.

I paid attention to how he inter-acted with Kent, as well as with me, for a few more days. Then I had the key. Whenever Cordy was taller than his people, he was in charge—dominant. As soon as one of us humans assumed our normal, upright stance and towered over Cordy, he lost dominance and became biddable. Therefore, for a couple of weeks while Kent and I established dominance, neither of us allowed Cordy to sit or stand so his head was higher than ours. Now, many months later, Cordy knows exactly who's who as far as the dominance hierarchy goes in the Wrede family. Kent can roughhouse with him yet determine how far the game goes and when it stops. I can play with Cordy and not get smacked with big feet or pushed around. He's still a very dominant dog, which I like, but he knows that he *must* obey his people.

If you have a dog that defies you, you haven't established your domi-nance yet. The first rule of estab-lishing your dominance is follow-through. Your dog *must* carry out every command that you give, assuming it knows what the com-

mand means. The more dominant the dog, the more important it is that you demand complete cooper-ation. Letting the dog get away once or twice with ignoring a com-mand it knows is a recipe for losing control at the most basic level. Oh, Cordy was a total crack-up as a clumsy puppy pretending he didn't know how to get into the station wagon, but what if I *had* to have him get into that vehicle and he fooled around? So a trip in the wagon always occurred when both Kent and I were present to force the issue physically until Cordy learned that "get into the car" meant "do it now, and don't horse around!"

In the pack situation, young dogs looked to older dogs for lessons on what it means to be a dog. If people don't give their dogs such lessons, the dog grows up any which way, uncontrolled, unpredictable, and

This five-week-old Rottweiler puppy wants to know who's boss and will thrive under loving training.

Your puppy looks to you for leadership.

unhappy. It may well end up at a shelter. Your job as owner of any dog is to teach it who's who. You're the boss. The dog is the dog—a valued companion and perhaps a worker, but not your superior.

Again I urge you to get to an obedience class. Experienced trainers will give you valuable lessons in how to work out the dominance issue without turning your feisty, happy dog into a cowering bundle of quivers.

And what if the dog you got *is* a cowering bundle of quivers? It's dominance again, but this time, too little. Shelter dogs particularly may have been abused at some time. Your job here is to build confidence in your dog. Do this by giving your dog lots of cheerful praise. Here it doesn't matter whether the dog understands your words if your voice and body language convey praise, joy, and confidence. Barbara Woodhouse, that great English dog trainer, used her joyous

"*What* a good dog!" to jolly even the most timid dog into becoming a happy camper.

With the timid dog, also be aware of your size compared to the dog's size. Stoop or squat to praise and/or approach your dog while you're in the confidence-building process so you don't loom over and threaten your dog.

Be especially patient with dogs from animal shelters. The reasons for fine dogs to be in shelters and available for adoption are numerous, strange, and often frivolous. "I'm moving to a new place and can't keep the dog," is all too common. When you consider a dog turned in for that reason, you're likely to be looking at a fine dog who got a bad roll of the dice on its first home and who will respond wonderfully to your love and training. If you find a dog that responds well to you in the chaotic climate of a busy animal shelter, you can bet that when you give that dog a happy home, you'll see canine blossoming you never dreamed of!

Beware of . . .

Don't let impulse or sympathy rule your good sense! Stick to the guidelines you've established for what you want your dog to be. I was bitterly sorry for the chows that ended up miserably at the shelter yearning for their one-and-only masters, but my style does not lend itself to one-person dogs like chows, so I searched for suitable homes for those chows, knowing mine isn't. Although it's true that the dog you perhaps want at a shelter may not be there another day, many shelters will hold a dog in a sort of informal way if you tell the personnel that you need to think the adoption over. Certainly if you're getting an adult dog from a breeder, you'll have the time to go away and think the choice over. People who place adult dogs generally know that it's in any dog's best interests to go to a permanent home, not out on whim, for many adult dogs have already had one bad experience with people. Take your time, for with a good match between you and your dog, you'll spend a lot of time together.

In a well-fenced yard, greyhounds can run to their hearts' content.

Chapter 7
Local Resources for Help

There are any number of excellent books on caring for puppies and dogs, and I'll note a few of my favorites in the Resources section (page 91). However, there are times when there's nothing like a face-to-face talk with a knowledgeable human to clarify a situation or solve a problem. If you're raising a puppy for one of the specialized organizations like Canine Companions for Independence, you have ample access to human resource people. If you got your dog or puppy from a careful local breeder,

Your dog's veterinarian is one of its best friends.

you've got built-in help. But there are other people who will partner with you as guides on bringing your new dog along so you both can live successfully together. I've been wonderfully helped by any number of "doggy" resource people. Let me suggest that you look to some of the following:

1. The veterinarian you choose
2. A local breeder of dogs either of the same breed as yours or of similar breeds
3. A professional dog trainer
4. Groomers
5. Professional handlers
6. Ethical pet store owners
7. Kennel clubs

Your Veterinarian

I was astonished recently when a young veterinarian told me that many people have an adversarial relationship with their dogs' vets. That's got to be the dumbest behavior there is! In a long life with dogs, I've met only three veterinarians I

chose not ever to take my dogs to, and of those three, only one did I disqualify on the basis of incompetence. Of the other two, one was unwilling (or unable?) to communicate clearly with me, the dog's owner; and the other went overboard on unnecessary procedures and aggressively pushed an expensive line of dog food as the only possible acceptable diet for any dog.

My dogs' vets have saved lives, done heroic operations in the witching hours, restored my sanity, taught me how to do simple but necessary procedures, opened their knowledge to me as I needed it, rapped me on the knuckles when I was being dumb, and treated me gently when I had just had to part with a dear old dog. Life with dogs would be grim for me if I didn't have access to well-educated, caring vets. I view them as my dogs' best friends, after Kent and me.

It is vital to feel comfortable with the vet who is going to be in charge of your dog's health. I recommend shopping for a veterinarian at least as carefully as you shop for your own family doctor. Ask dog-owning friends whom they use and why. If your dog came from a local breeder, at least try out the vet that breeder uses. I think sadly of John who took his Dane puppy to vet after vet, all out of our local area, for what was finally diagnosed as a really simple condition, easily remedied. By the time John got to the vet who made the correct diagnosis, he had spent thousands of dollars, put his dog through severe treatments, and ultimately degraded the quality of his dog's life. The miracle-working veterinarian turned out to be a good friend of George, the vet I had recommended to John in the first place. George consulted with the other vet regularly on the man's specialty, but John was one of those people who can never believe that the local yokels really know anything, so how could he bring himself to use the vet I used?

Because most veterinary care takes place in the dog's home, vets have to know how to impress upon the owner the exact procedures that must be done at home. Hence, communication skills are vital. But communication is a two-way deal. Owners must take seriously what their veterinarians tell them, ask questions, and be clear on what they're supposed to do. Since many of us get frazzled when our dog is sick, it's smart to write down what the vet tells you, so you aren't depending on a memory that left for Tierra del Fuego the minute the vet said, "Surgery." The most important skill you can build is clear, open communication with the veterinarian you choose. Half of this equation is your clear, specific description of what you've seen that makes you think your dog is sick. The other half is your listening to what the vet tells you after examining your dog. The more you show concerned interest, the more your vet is going to help you understand your dog's health issues.

Good vets are interested first in good health for their patients. This means that they consider diet, parasites, immunizations, spaying or neutering, and proper hygiene all as factors bearing on a dog's health. Many behavior problems stem from health problems, and often your vet can help you ferret out what's wrong. It's smart, as I said before, to go to your chosen veterinarian for a consultation shortly after you get your dog, and it's fair to expect to pay for that consultation, for you're gaining valuable information. Feel free to ask questions. "Should I be worried about gastric torsion, Doctor?" is a valid and important question to raise, just as it's smart to ask about any unusual problems the vet knows about in dogs of the breed you've chosen. Be diligent about reading any printed material the vet gives you. More and more, all of us are learning that wellness is more than the absence of disease. Veterinarians have been ahead of people doctors on this issue for years. As we learn new things, some of our cherished lore becomes obsolete. Be open to the scholarship your veterinarian brings to your dog's quality of life.

When you find the right veterinarian for your dog and you, you're looking at a partner, not an adversary!

Beware of . . .

- Veterinarians who insist that the only nutritious dog food in the world is the brand they happen to sell. This behavior is a flag that warns of more interest in money than in health and knowledge. Yes, vets do sell food, and that's a legitimate aspect of their business, but they ought not to be hucksters.
- A veterinarian who never corrects any of your misconceptions. If you're doing something against your dog's best interests, your vet is correct in telling you so—is, in fact, doing you a favor. So get your ego on leash and listen up.
- A vet who won't answer your questions in plain language. Kent got irate at a vet who talked such scientific gibberish that he couldn't figure out what day of the week it was, let alone what was going on with his dog. Needless to say that vet didn't get any more of the Wrede pet business.
- A vet who appears not to like dogs.

Local Dog Breeders

Next to veterinarians, nobody has seen as many dog disasters as a longtime, serious dog breeder. When it comes to puppy problems, these folks have seen 'em all! Generally they work closely with the vet of their choice, and many of them stay current on newly discovered health problems and nutrition guidelines for their breed. Most of them are slightly unbalanced on the subject of their favorite breed of dogs, and they beam upon others who are brilliant enough to have discovered the wonders of, say, Great Danes.

Thus, even if you got your Swamphound when you were in Maine and now you're in Oregon, the chances are good that if you approach a local breeder of Swamphounds in a friendly way, you'll be welcomed as one of the family. Make your first approach by phone. No breeder welcomes a stranger who shows up right in the middle of cleaning puppy pens. If you're having a problem with your dog, ask whether the breeder can guide you on what to do. The chances are that you'll be invited to bring your dog for a visit. When you do so, be a good guest and don't assume that because the breeder already has a bazillion Swamphounds, yours is welcome to run loose on the place. Keep the visit focused; this may mean that your children stay home this time. (There are many dog breeders who do not dote on children.)

Egos get in the way when people are comparing dogs. A kind breeder will talk up your dog's strong points and perhaps only mention weaknesses in passing and if urged to do so. If you take one look at this breeder's dogs and realize that there's a stark lack of quality, murmur nice nothings and leave as soon as it's polite. Neither of you owes the other an adoption! If, on

the other hand, you find a gold mine of knowledge, quality, and friendliness, you're in luck. Even if your dog is, truly, a sorry example of the breed, any decent breeder loves you for having seen the splendid qualities of Swamphounds and will work with you to make the most of what you have. Walt came to us with Chinook, the ugliest young male Dane I've ever seen. He wanted to buy a bitch to breed Chinook to! Well, Walt is one of the neatest people I've met, a dog person through and through. And in spite of his physical faults, Chinook was a Dane in the best sense as far as his temperament went. To the shows he'd never go, nor should he have passed on his multiplicity of physical defects, but Chinook knew how to treat his people and be a Dane. After traveling to a few shows with us (sans Chinook), Walt recognized that his dog was a one-and-only and had Chinook neutered. Kent and I still laugh

Curious Australian cattle puppies.

when we review Chinook stories, and he, Walt, and the blue bitch Walt always referred to as "Ole Fireball" had a great life together.

If there isn't a breeder locally who raises your breed, look for one who specializes in something close. Breeders of tiny dogs know the idiosyncrasies of the littles. Hound breeders know hounds. You get the picture. There's a tendency there—it probably is true that people are a lot like the dogs they choose to live with, and hence they tend to like other people who have chosen similar dogs. So you can get taken under the wing of a breeder of Fenhounds, who will know some of the special needs of the Swamphound.

From such a person you'll learn what local vet specializes in your kind of dog, what local dog trainers understand Swamphounds, who the good handlers in the area are, what some of the breed problems are—and how to handle them.

Beware of . . .

- A badmouther. If there were never any decent Swamphounds except the ones produced by this person's stock, take your leave and keep your distance.
- A puppymiller. Careful, ethical breeders realize that it takes years to learn all the ins and outs of one breed. Maybe it's possible to know both beagles and bassetts thoroughly, but I bet it takes more study than most people have time for to know beagles, bassets, cocker spaniels, poodles, and rottweilers all well enough to be doing the breeds a service rather than just mass-producing puppies for the bucks. Give a wide berth to the breeder who is doing assembly-line puppy production.
- A breeder who doesn't have any old dogs on the place. What happens to the oldsters when their days in the show ring or the puppy box are done? How can you know your breed if you don't know them when they're old?
- Breeders who do major veterinary procedures themselves. I even question breeders who are too cheap to get their puppies immunized by a veterinarian, as skimping here can indicate a general attitude of "do it on the cheap." The breeding of purebred dogs is not a money-maker, and although breeders do have to be careful of how they spend their money, the well-being of their dogs should not suffer.

Dog Trainers

The business section of any telephone directory will yield you access to various dog trainers and/or dog training clubs. Most hold classes for groups of dogs; some also offer individualized training. I prefer group sessions. Dogs need to be socialized, not only with people, but also with other dogs.

They also need to learn to perform and behave under stressful and distracting circumstances. Finally, owners need to learn to control their dogs. Every one of us benefits in some way by being a member of a training class. I knew some boxer owners who sent their boxer away to an obedience school because he was surly and out of control. Well, he graduated from the school all right, but when he came home, he behaved the same way he always had. And no wonder—his owners hadn't bothered to learn the skills dog trainers teach. There are some things you cannot just throw money at, and dog training is one of them. Those boxer people spent a small fortune to have their dog trained, but the only people he worked for were the trainers—with whom he did not live!

Once you find out when and where obedience classes are being held, go visit without your dog. You want to find out whether the training methods suit your needs, how large the classes are, how much individual attention the dogs get, and how skilled the trainer is. If your visit is discouraged, scratch that trainer! But you shouldn't be surprised or put off because visiting dogs are discouraged. There's a limit to the chaos anyone can stand.

What I look for in a training situation are these:

1. Insistence that all dogs be fully immunized
2. A multi-breed class
3. Dogs broken out into groups reflecting age and ability
4. No inhumane methods used, including a ban on spiked or pronged collars
5. A class small enough that the dogs have room to work
6. A trainer willing to be hands-on
7. A trainer who insists on proper behavior and equipment
8. Praise/reward training methods

There are stubborn dogs that take a strong training hand, and a competent trainer knows who they are. However, there are as many dogs that can be broken by a strong hand, and a trainer must know that, too. Any situation where I see dogs cowering away from a trainer is one into which I won't take any of my dogs. In truth, most of the dog trainers I've known have loved dogs and wanted nothing more than to help as many of them as possible become good canine citizens through basic obedience training.

Dogs on the Down/Stay in obedience class.

Basic obedience is, I think, good for all dogs. I noted with interest that all the special-needs dogs go through a basic obedience training before their more specialized lessons. If one becomes excited about obedience work, there are several advanced degrees one can pursue, including the rigorous tracking course. But first steps first!

Many trainers won't take puppies under six months old. I see their point, because the youngsters have relatively short attention spans. However, I've chosen to live with giants who, by six months, can drag small people over the horizon, so I like short training courses for puppies from about four months to a year old. Half-hour sessions are enough, and I don't look for much work off the leash at this time. It's enough to get the little ones heeling, sitting, staying, downing, and coming.

Since most of the canine problems that drive people crazy aren't covered by basic obedience work, I like trainers who offer problem-solving sessions along with the basic obedience work. Indeed, it was because of those maddening problems that I began accumulating the material that finally comprised my book *Civilizing Your Puppy*. Nor do dogs suddenly quit doing crazy things when they become adults by some calendar definition. A trainer who doesn't know that doesn't know dogs!

Beware of . . .

- Attack training. Responsible dog trainers know how few people are physically or temperamentally suited to owning an attack dog, and they discourage such training. The ruination of many macho breeds of dogs has been accomplished by macho trainers of both sexes who try to make the dogs into vicious weapons. Just this week I heard of a woman who had her rottweiler attack-trained.

  "Does she know dogs well?" I asked the person who told me.

  "This is her first dog."

  "Is she calm, strong, and dominant?" I asked next.

  "No. She's fluttery, slight, and scatterbrained."

  And some scam-artist took $1,500 from this woman to turn what might have been a perfectly manageable rott into a liability.
- Aversion training. It is the rare dog that needs electric shocks, pronged collars, electric prods, or other extreme punishments to learn to behave. So rare are these dogs that I'd guess such a dog might more properly be euthanized than punished into a sort of uneasy truce with the human race.
- Classes where sick dogs are welcome.
- Classes where cruelty of any kind from any source is tolerated. Owners who are cruel to their dogs should be firmly taught other methods of control and behavior.

Groomers

Knowledgeable dog groomers will not only help you keep your dog looking good, they can guide you on proper diet and lead you to other professionals in the local dog world. Many veterinarians have groomers working in their clinics, and many groomers are avid students of dogs. Some professional handlers of show dogs supplement their incomes by grooming dogs.

If you find an honest groomer, you'll also learn more than you may want to know about your dog's temperament. I say "honest" because, with all the egotism involved with people and their dogs, lots of groomers avoid telling owners that their little darling is hell on wheels on the grooming table. My friend Eileen did a lot of grooming, and I used to get upset with her when she lied to people about how their dogs behaved. She'd be delivering a fluffy, clean, beribboned little froufrou dog that, an hour ago, had been trying to take her face off, and she'd say to the owner, "Oh, she was just a little doll!" I maintain that the owner deserved to know what a jerk her dog had been, and a recent scan of grooming ads tells me I'm correct. I see ads announcing, "No tranquilizers used." Aha! So the new wrinkle is to zonk the little wretches.

Work on developing honesty between you and whatever groomer you choose. You need to know whether your dog challenges people

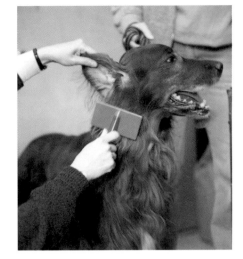

A nice Irish setter enjoying a grooming session.

who are doing things for it, because you need to know how your dog acts under stress. In our litigious times, you can afford another obedience class or a muzzle a lot better than you can a lawsuit for dog bites.

A good groomer will also teach you how to maintain your dog in between visits for The Works. Getting some of the little tricks of the trade helps you do the job better and more quickly.

Beware of . . .

- A groomer who tries to supplant your veterinarian.
- A groomer who tries to load you up with merchandise.
- A groomer who won't teach you anything.
- A groomer your dog doesn't like. How much force is being used when you're not around?
- A groomer who doesn't insist that your dog be properly immunized.

87

Handlers

Generally you'll need the services of a dog handler only if you're going to show your dog. However, should you find yourself in a place where there's no breeder who knows your breed, look for an all-breed handler. Dog trainers would know of local handlers, as would groomers and perhaps your veterinarian. Many handlers once bred dogs, and the all-breed handler knows at least what a good Swamphound should look like. I've learned a lot from handlers, even though I seldom sent my dogs into the ring under a professional. Most valuable were the pointers on flying dogs and puppies, which I got from two great old handlers who had never lost a dog. I also learned the proper way to cut a dog's nails from a handler, and the importance of teaching a dog to go into a crate. I got a tip on which boarding kennel was clean and well run from a handler. Lots of handlers run conformation classes, in which they teach owners how to show their dogs to best advantage.

Beware of . . .

The handler that tries to hustle you! Yes, handlers make their money showing dogs, and if you do have an outstanding dog, any sensible handler will itch to take it into the ring. Before letting your dog go off on a show circuit with any handler, however, go to some dog shows and observe how that handler treats dogs when away from home. I spent a lot of time being an inconspicuous tourist where the handlers park their elaborate rigs at dog shows, and I learned who stuffed their dogs into crates and never took them out for exercise, and who sent younger dogs less likely to win big into the show ring with an exercise person while charging full-bore as if they'd done the job they were being paid for. By the time I had dogs ready for a handler, I knew who was a real dog lover and who was a showboater.

In the obedience ring, only family members are allowed as handlers.

Pet Store Owners

As I said earlier, responsible pet store owners tend to be real animal lovers. They know a lot about the local dog scene, for they get asked to donate to pet fairs, fun matches, and local dog shows. Many of them have made themselves expert on canine nutrition and carry excellent dog foods. Generally they're a much better source of dog food than supermarkets. Best of all, these folks know who on the local dog scene is caring well for their dogs and who is getting by on the cheap, so if you ask the right questions the right way, over time you'll get a fund of information.

Not only can you find a wide range of nutritious foods in a good pet store, you'll be able to choose the right equipment for your dog, from collars and obedience leashes to beds, toys, and specialized items like advanced obedience retrieval dumbbells. Most carry the most complete stock of dog books you're likely to find. Their bulletin boards will inform you of local canine events and lead you to a network of the doggy people you want to know.

Kennel Clubs

Most large cities have at least one all-breed kennel club. If the club isn't listed in your phone book, groomers and dog trainers are likely to know how to contact the right person. The purpose of most kennel clubs is to put on fun matches and dog shows. Most are perennially short of willing workers, so if you want to learn about dog shows from the inside out, here's the chance to do so.

In a kennel club you'll see people at their best and worst. I've always been impressed at dog shows at how well the dogs behave and how badly many of their owners do! If the dogs savaged each other the way many owners verbally slash at each other, shows would be a bloody mess. And yet I've also met some very helpful people at shows and through kennel clubs. As long as you're aware that politics is the name of the game in most kennel clubs, you'll be all right. At their best, kennel clubs hold classes teaching people how to show their dogs, and seminars on nutrition and important health issues. They work with local animal control personnel to be sure beneficial animal ordinances are passed and enforced, and they lobby hard against legislation unfriendly to dogs. They close ranks against puppy millers and pass the word on dirty boarding kennels or unfit trainers. If you're a serious dog fancier, you will find club members to take you under their wing.

At their worst, kennel clubs are factionalized hotbeds of gossip and backstabbing. Fortunately, such behavior is counterproductive, so either a new faction reins in the ugliness, or the kennel club dissolves into its warring factions, out of which eventually a new club rises.

Besides the all-breed clubs, there are specialized clubs. If you live in a large city, there is likely to be a Greater Metropolis Swamphound Club. Other breed clubs may operate on a regional basis. There are specialized clubs at every level of obedience work. Some clubs widen their scope to include several breeds that all do more or less the same thing, as with terrier trials, for instance, or field trials for sporting dogs. These are generally sponsored by some umbrella club dedicated to the advancement of the dogs they've chosen. There is, to me, something wonderfully honest about a terrier who goes down the hole and gets the rat, as it was bred to do. Or the Weimaraner who quarters the field and finds the one and only bird there, and the bloodhound whose nose leads it unerringly to the person it is tracking. The people who conscientiously keep their dogs true to their original jobs are the ones who didn't get carried away by a dazzle of ribbons and silver coasters at some bench show where all a dog has to do is look pretty.

* * *

You may choose exactly the right dog and never need any of the resources I've talked about here except your veterinarian. But it's comforting to know there's a big network of folks out there who are dedicated to the idea that people and dogs can live very nicely together and who are ready to help make that a reality.

A border collie that is trained to work sheep is priceless on a ranch.

Appendix
Other Resources

Organizations

The American Kennel Club
5580 Centerview Drive, Suite 200
Raleigh, NC 27606-3390

This is the premier dog registration organization in the U.S. Purebred dogs are registered with the AKC, and from them you can find out whether a breed is recognized in the U.S.

Canine Companions
for Independence
1215 Sebastopol Road
Santa Rosa, CA 95407
(707) 579-1985

From these folks you can learn about dogs for people who have mobility problems, as well as hearing dogs for the deaf. You might want, instead, to find out about becoming a puppyraiser family, a volunteer, or a donor.

Delta Society
Century Building, Suite 303
321 Burnett Ave., So.
Renton, WA 98055
(206) 226-7357

For $3, you can get an up-to-date directory of organizations that do special training with dogs or provide dogs for special purposes.

Dogs for the Deaf, Inc.
10175 Wheeler Road
Central Point, OR 97502
(503) 826-9220 Voice/TDD

This is one of the organizations that rescues unwanted dogs from animal shelters and trains them to be hearing dogs. You might volunteer to be a puppy raiser for them, or you might know someone who needs one of their dogs.

Guide Dogs for the Blind, Inc.
350 Los Ranchitos Road
San Rafael, CA 94915-1200
(415) 499-4000

This is the oldest and best-known of the organizations that train specialty dogs. Like the others, they need volunteers, donors, and puppy raiser families.

Books

Anderson, Robert, DVM, and Barbara J. Wrede: *Caring for Older Cats & Dogs* (Williamson, Charlotte, Vermont, 1990). With guidance on nutrition, attention to what to watch for in the aging process, and material on starting a puppy out right, this book gives you the spectrum of canine care.

Baer, Ted: *Communicating with Your Dog* (Barron's, Hauppauge, New York, 1989). Shows you how to bring your dog along step by step on learning commands. Very good on not confusing your dog by teaching too much too soon.

Lorenz, Konrad: *King Solomon's Ring* (Crowell, 1952). You'll get valuable insights into how animals think, especially useful for your future with dogs.

_____ *Man Meets Dog* (Penguin, 1965). This is a great key to the mind of a dog. Here's a book that can teach you really to think like a dog, which is one of the most important factors in living happily with canines.

Mowat, Farley: *Never Cry Wolf* (Bantam, 1983). Dispelling many myths about wolves, Mowat gives you another look into how the canine mind works.

Pearsall, Milo, and Charles G. Leedham: *Dog Obedience Training* (Charles Scribner's Sons, 1979). This book is tops on training methods that work without breaking your dog's spirit.

Visualizations of the Dog Standards (Popular Dogs Publishing Company). Get the most recent edition available if you're buying this one, because it'll remain a classic reference for you for years. Here you can see all the recognized breeds and read the breed standards which the dogs are supposed to conform to. You might regard this as your "shopping guide" to dogs.

Wrede, Barbara J.: *Civilizing Your Puppy* (Barron's, Hauppauge, New York, 1992). Here you have the field-tested methods that make living with a dog the joy it shoud be. Deals with forming good habits and breaking bad ones, which you'll need if you get an adult dog.

Index